Ancestors of David Garland Edwards

Generation 1

1.   **David Garland Edwards**, son of Roy Garland Edwards and Maribel Savage was born on 21 May 1945 in Fort Sumner, New Mexico. He married **Hope Ellen Stewart**, daughter of Robert McDaniel Stewart and Phyllis Olene Tucker on 09 Mar 1968 in Tampa, Florida. She was born on 27 Jun 1949 in South Perry, Ohio.

More About David Garland Edwards:
Military Service: Bet. Nov 1965-Nov 1967; U.S. Army

Generation 2

2.   **Roy Garland Edwards**, son of LeRoy Ardis Edwards and Emma Georgie Irene Garland was born on 30 May 1922 in Loraine, Texas. He died on 14 Oct 1974 in Tampa, Florida. He married **Maribel Savage**, daughter of William Payne Savage and Mary Bell Badgett on 08 Apr 1944 in Lubbock, Texas.

3.   **Maribel Savage**, daughter of William Payne Savage and Mary Bell Badgett was born on 22 Jun 1926 in Sherman, Texas. She died on 14 Feb 2010 in Tampa, Florida.

More About Roy Garland Edwards:
Burial: 17 Oct 1974 in Pleasant Grove Cemetery, Durant, Florida Cause Of Death: Heart Failure
Occupation: 1940 in Olton, Texas; Repairman
Military Service: Bet. 1942-1964; U.S. Air Force (Major)

Notes for Roy Garland Edwards:
Died at the base hospital on MacDill Air Force Base.

More About Maribel Savage:
Burial: 18 Feb 2010 in Pleasant Grove Cemetery, Durant, Florida

Notes for Maribel Savage:
Born Mary Bell Savage but known as Maribel most of her life. Original birth certificate does not have a first name and amended birth certificate, filed June 20, 1952, has Maribel for her first name

Maribel Savage and Roy Garland Edwards had the following children:

1.   i.   David Garland Edwards, son of Roy Garland Edwards and Maribel Savage was born on 21 May 1945 in Fort Sumner, New Mexico. He married Hope Ellen Stewart, daughter of Robert McDaniel Stewart and Phyllis Olene Tucker on 09 Mar 1968 in Tampa, Florida. She was born on 27 Jun 1949 in South Perry, Ohio.

    ii.   Robert Marion Edwards, son of Roy Garland Edwards and Maribel Savage was born on 11 Dec 1946 in Lubbock, Texas. He died on 13 Feb 2010 in San Francisco, California. He met Catherine Vlachos. She was born on 07 May 1950. She died on 17 Oct 2001 in San Francisco, California.

More About Robert Marion Edwards:
Cause Of Death: Lung Cancer

Notes for Robert Marion Edwards:

Never Married.

More About Catherine Vlachos:
Burial: Ohio
Cause Of Death: Cancer

Notes for Catherine Vlachos:
Robert and Catherine (Cathy) were not married but lived together a number
of years until her death.

<hr>

Generation 3

4.   **LeRoy Ardis Edwards**, son of Ambrose Newton Edwards and Joanna Columbia Ardis was born
       on 27 Feb 1881 in Sulphur Springs, Texas. He died on 05 Dec 1951 in Loraine, Texas. He
       married **Emma Georgie Irene Garland**, daughter of Edward Warren Garland and Julia Rebecca
       Kimbell on 27 Jul 1921 in Roscoe, Texas.

5.   **Emma Georgie Irene Garland**, daughter of Edward Warren Garland and Julia Rebecca Kimbell
       was born on 23 Mar 1880 in Annona, Texas. She died on 17 Dec 1969 in Kerrville, Texas.

More About LeRoy Ardis Edwards:
Burial: 07 Dec 1951 in Loraine Cemetery, Loraine,
Texas Cause Of Death: Carcinoma of Lung
Occupation: 1910 in Brazoria County, Texas; Truck Farmer
Occupation: 1918 in Ranger, Eastland County, Texas; Manager of Buell Lumber
Company
Occupation: 1920 in Loraine, Texas; Lumber Yard Manager
Occupation: 1930 in Loraine, Texas; Lumber Yard Manager
Occupation: 1940 in Olton, Texas; Retail Lumber Yard Manager
Occupation: 1942 in Olton, Lamb County, Texas; Manager of Higgingbotham Lumber

Company Notes for LeRoy Ardis Edwards:

       Discovered and operated, with his brother Walter, "Baking Powder" gold mine
near Rosedale, New Mexico.

     Dear Mr. Edwards:
     Your request to our Geological Information Center for information on the Baking Powder
mine was forwarded to me. Probably fewer than a half-dozen living people in all the southwest
have even heard of
this property as it is one of the more obscure such in all New Mexico. I am not aware that the
property was ever examined by a trained geologist or engineer (unless your Edwards relatives
were such and there is no known surviving record of their work). My extensive mines and
prospects files are absolutely silent in regard to the Baking Powder. Nevertheless I have noted
one or two very obscure references in my research.
     The Baking Powder is located in the Rosedale Mining District at the extreme north end of the San
Mateo mountains in southern Socorro county, New Mexico. I have not examined the mining claim
records in the local courthouse for exact dates (mainly because you are the very first individual to
ever request information on the property!) but would predict the claim (or claims) was

located during latter part of the 19th century -- poss. mid-1890s -- as a result of the success of the well-known Rosedale mine and discovery of the nearby White Cap.

The "veins" in the Rosedale district are actually brecciated shear zones in the volcanic (rhyolitic) rocks The brecciated and sheared rhyolite has been recemented with a hard, bluish-white quartz and later with a clearer vein-type quartz. The entire vein mass is highly silicified and in those areas yielding the best gold values are heavily stained with the black and red oxides of manganese and iron respectively. Gold occurred in the native state in the upper oxidized portions of the vein but is very nearly absent in the sulfide portion at or below the water table. Remarkably, little or no silver is present. I would predict the Baking Powder "vein" to be similar in character to the above. Dr. Charles Ferguson's doctoral dissertation covered a large area extending from the southern end of the Rosedale District to the north well beyond White Cap and Big Rosa canyons. I asked Charlie if he knew the locality of the Baking Powder and other prospects and he indicated approximate locations for two unnamed mine workings about two miles north and northwest of the Rosedale which I feel are the White Cap and the Baking Powder. The projected location for the latter is approx. Sec3, T6S, R6W near the head of Big Rosa canyon.

Soon after the turn of the century, development on the Baking Powder had apparently progressed to the mining stage. According to a note in the Engineering and Mining Journal, 24 December 1903, p 988, the Baking Powder mine was said to be initiating "full operations," whatever that meant; Walter Edwards, undoubtedly your ancestor, was the manager. Unfortunately the operation failed to live up to expectations and within four years was facing foreclosure for $1200 in back wages (Soccoro Chieftan, 30 November 1907). The obvious conclusion is that the mine failed to develop pay ore in sufficient quantities to sustain the operation and it failed. And that is the current extent of the "historic" record!

I and my colleagues attempted to visit this prospect in May 2000, but despite our "approximate" location on the topo sheet, and a full day's search, four-wheeling, etc., we failed to locate it. I should note that the 'road' up Big Rosa canyon is, in places, a figment of the imagination -- we could have easily missed a small prospect off in the ponderosas! The Mount Whithington jeep road may pass within a mile of the mine on the west and that is the route I will next attempt.

Now that you have made a request for information, I shall keep a sharp lookout for additional data. I must yet peruse the pages of the few issues of the San Marcial Bee that have survived the ravages of time and will keep you in mind should anything materialize. Additionally I will examine the claim location records upon my next visit to the courthouse. On the other hand, I'd be most pleased to add to our archival files any information you'd be willing to share with us from your family's papers. Regards,
Robert W. Eveleth Senior
Mining Engineer Curator,
Mining Archives

Dear Mr. Edwards:

Recent research on several articles of local mining interest has, once again, led me through the pages of the Socorro Chieftain. Recalling your interest in the above, I made a copy of an article on the Baking Powder/Edwards Bros., reproduced below in its entirety:

Socorro Chieftain, 6/14/1902, p 4: "Rosedale, N. M., June 10m, 1902 -- Editor Chieftain -- Rosedale is quiet at present. Big Rosa, 2-1/2 miles to the northwest, shows great and rapidly increasing activity. Fully $5,000 worth of work is now underway and other contracts are being let. The immediate cause of this work was the discovery and partial development of the Baking Powder property of the Edwards Brothers of El Paso, Tex. This claim showed well from the surface but now at a depth of 55 feet it is exciting old time prospectors and tenderfeet alike by yielding a strong vein of high grade ore while picked samples show as high as 84 ounces in gold. Two or more stamp mills, stores, drink emporiums, a post office, dozens of cabins and tents, a good graded road up Big Rosa, and a couple of hundred men tearing into its mountain sides may be a vision, but as a miner and prospector of long experience I think this and more will be a reality within 12 months. Big Rosa may not be as good a mining camp as Cripple Creek, Colo. It may be better. The writer has no interest there and is not puffing the camp to "induce capital," but is sincere in saying that right now is a suitable and very favorable time to investigate Big Rosa.

There can be no harm in keeping an eye on the indicator." Signed: A. L. Heister."

As I continue to go through the pages of the Socorro Chieftan, I'll be sure to let you know if the writer's dream materialized.

Best Regards,
Robert W. Eveleth
Senior Mining Engineer

--- ----

More About Emma Georgie Irene Garland:
Burial: 20 Dec 1969 in Loraine Cemetery, Loraine, Texas
Cause Of Death: Broncho Pneumonia and Arteriosclerosis

More About LeRoy Ardis Edwards and Emma Georgie Irene Garland:
Marriage License: 27 Jul 1921 in Mitchell County, Texas
Marriage Fact: Married by S. H. Young, M.G.

Emma Georgie Irene Garland and LeRoy Ardis Edwards had the following child:
2.   i. Roy Garland Edwards, son of LeRoy Ardis Edwards and Emma Georgie Irene Garland was born on 30 May 1922 in Loraine, Texas. He died on 14 Oct 1974 in Tampa, Florida. He married Maribel Savage, daughter of William Payne Savage and Mary Bell Badgett on 08 Apr 1944 in Lubbock, Texas. She was born on 22 Jun 1926 in Sherman, Texas. She died on 14 Feb 2010 in Tampa, Florida.

6.   **William Payne Savage** was born on 23 Sep 1903 in Whitewright, Texas. He died in Jul 1970 in Oklahoma City, Oklahoma. He married **Mary Bell Badgett** on 28 Feb 1925.

7.   **Mary Bell Badgett** was born on 19 Oct 1905 in Bells, Texas. She died on 20 Feb 1964 in Houston, Texas.

More About Mary Bell Badgett:

Burial: Quitaque, Texas

Mary Bell Badgett and William Payne Savage had the following child:
3.   i. Maribel Savage, daughter of William Payne Savage and Mary Bell Badgett was born on 22 Jun 1926 in Sherman, Texas. She died on 14 Feb 2010 in Tampa, Florida. She married Roy Garland Edwards, son of LeRoy Ardis Edwards and Emma Georgie Irene Garland on 08 Apr 1944 in Lubbock, Texas. He was born on 30 May 1922 in Loraine, Texas. He died on 14 Oct 1974 in Tampa, Florida.

Generation 4

8.   **Ambrose Newton Edwards**, son of Ambrose Edwards and Emeline James Gaulding was born on 21 Oct 1840 in Russell County, Alabama. He died on 20 Jul 1933 in Strawn, Texas. He married **Joanna Columbia Ardis**, daughter of Isaac Ardis and Jane Elizabeth White on 05 Dec 1865 in Dale County, Alabama.

9.   **Joanna Columbia Ardis**, daughter of Isaac Ardis and Jane Elizabeth White was born on 04 Feb 1847 in Salem, Alabama. She died on 08 Aug 1922 in Greenville, Texas.

More About Ambrose Newton Edwards:
Burial: 21 Jul 1933 in Forest Park Cemetery, Greenville, Texas- Moved later to Restland Cemetery, Dallas, Texas
Cause Of Death: Prostate Cancer
Occupation: 1860 in Dale County, Alabama; School Teacher

Occupation: 1870 in Sulphur Springs, Texas; Dry Goods Merchant
Occupation: 1880 in Hopkins County, Texas; County Clerk
Occupation: Bet. 27 Mar 1886-20 Oct 1891 ; Postmaster, Eliasville,
Texas Occupation: 1900 in Palo Pinto County, Texas; Lumber Dealer
Occupation: 1910 in Gordon, Palo Pinto County, Texas; Lumber
Merchant
Occupation: 1920 in Palo Pinto County, Texas; Retired
Occupation: 1930 in Greenville, Texas; Retired - Living with his son, Ambrose Edwin Edwards
Military Service: Bet. 03 Jul 1861-11 Jun 1865 in C.S.A.; Company E, 15th Alabama Infantry

Notes for Ambrose Newton Edwards:
    Enlisted on July 3, 1861 in Westville, Alabama and served until July 2, 1863 when he was
captured at Gettysburg, Pennsylvania and made a prisoner of war. Sent first to Fort McHenry,
Maryland on July 5, 1863 and then to Fort Delaware, Delaware on July 6, 1863. Released
from Fort Delaware on June 11, 1865.

    Engagements: Winchester, Cross Keys, Harpers Ferry, Sharpsburg, Fredricksburg,
Suffolk, Malvern Hill, Cedar Mt. Hazel River, 2nd Manassas, Chantilly, Gettysburg.

    Wounded at Sharpsburg.and Fredricksburg.

    Promoted to Second Sergeant May 15, 1862.
    Promoted to First Sergeant July 25, 1862.
    Promoted to Second Lieutenant but was captured at Gettysburg, Pennsylvania before
his commission arrived.

    Pre Civil War Residence was Westville, Alabama.

    Flag of the Army of Northern Virginia covered his casket during his first funeral and burial
at Greeneville, Texas.

    Member of the first Board of Regents for the University of Texas 1881-1882

    Buried in Greenville, Texas in 1933 and then buried in Restland Cemetery, Dallas, Texas
on February 9, 1955, grave marker set on August 31, 1955.

    Became a Mason at Brightstar Lodge number 221 in Sulphur Springs, Texas on November
5, 1868.

    Death certificate gives October 18, 1840 as date of birth.

Dictated to Emma Irene Garland (Edwards) in 1930

    I well remember the day when my company assembled at old Darian Church in Dale
County, Alabama, where we bade good bye to our loved ones and took up our march to the
battle front in answer to our country's call.
    I remember the first night we camped on the banks of Pea River and bathed in its waters and
spent this our first night in joyous hilarity. I remember after three days march we reached old Fort
Mitchell near Columbus Georgia, where we were organized into the 15th Alabama Infantry, my
company being known as co. E. Then after a few weeks of company and regimental drill we had
orders to go to Virginia, and this was for me a matter of exquisite thrill and interest which cannot
be well depicted here.
    When we reached Richmond we were quartered at Old Chimborozo where we remained
about three weeks and thence to Manassas. Shortly after the noted first battle of the war, as
there was no more fighting in this section, we went into winter quarters there. Up to this time we
had not had to suffer any great hardships, but had many interesting experiences.
    In the beginning of 1862, the second year of the war, greater activities in war matters became
more tense. McClelland was assembling a great army in the Yorktown peninsula with the purpose

of marching on to Richmond and General Johnson was ordered to fall back from Manassas to meet this move of the enemy. But Ewell's division, to which I belonged, was ordered to join Stonewall Jackson in the valley. Then my regiment was in the noted Valley campaign in which Jackson defeated three armies and then it was at Cross Keys we received our baptism of battle. From here the scene changed and the Seven days battle around Richmond was fought in which my regiment took an active part and lost quite a number of noble men.

I was sick and in the hospital at Charlottesville at that time. After McClelland's defeat General Lee moved his army North. On the first invasion. we crossed the Potomac at Leesburg, wading it of course as there were no bridges. My division was ordered to go around and cross back above Harper's Ferry where General Wool was stationed with seven thousand men. We had him completely surrounded and he surrendered. In this surrender we secured arms, commissary, and quarter master supplies in great abundance.

Immediately after the surrender we were ordered back across the Potomac to be in the battle of Sharpsburg - called Antetim by the North Historians - this was one of the hardest battles of the war, and was known as a draw. Lee withdrew to the Virginia side and there ended that year's campaign in Virginia.

To avoid being tedious, I will omit many important military operations including the battle of Fredricksburg in which i took a part and will speak of the Pennsylvania invasion and the battle of Gettysburg. I was in this battle and on the second day of July 1863, with thirteen other men of my company was captured and carried to Fort Delaware where we were kept as prisoners until the war closed.

I could make an interesting chapter about our prison, but only say we managed to keep up spirit and hope amid its trials and troubles until the day came for our release nearly two months after the surrender.

I reached home on the 5th of June 1865, to find our beloved Southland wrecked and ruined by war's devastation.

Then it was with unflinching courage we took up the task of reconstructing the ruin and building our new South upon it. While I cannot elaborate on this work, for it would require many words, yet I cannot omit saying that the work was done in a way that solicited the admiration of all people. Our noble women were our staunch co-laborers in every sence, and deserve a monument for their wonderful work.

On the 5th of December 1865 it was my good fortune to lead to the marriage alter one of the best of the noble daughters of the South, to walk with me and share with me, every joy and every sorrow that awaited us on lifes pilgrimage. We came to Texas in 1866 where eight sons came to bless our union, all noble men and all living useful lives in Texas except one. Eight years ago my precious one left me to go and wear her crown.

Now in my 90th year I can truly say that much love and kindness have been meted out to me, but must say that the best friends we old veterans have are the noble Daughters of the Confederacy, and may god bless them in my closing word.

A. N. Edwards
Co. E. 15th Alabama Inf.

More About Joanna Columbia Ardis:
Burial: 08 Aug 1922 in Forest Park Cemetery, Greenville, Texas- Moved later to
Restland Cemetery, Dallas, Texas
Cause Of Death: Stomach Cancer

Notes for Joanna Columbia Ardis:
Re buried in Restland Cemetery, Dallas, Texas on February 9, 1955, grave marker set on August

----

Joanna Columbia Ardis and Ambrose Newton Edwards had the following children:

i. Isaac Mansfield Edwards, son of Ambrose Newton Edwards and Joanna Columbia Ardis was born on 01 Feb 1868 in Strawn, Texas. He died on 18 Mar 1945 in Strawn Texas. He married Mary Sophronia (Onie) Strawn, daughter of Stephen Bethel Strawn and Emeline Jane Allen in 1899 in Palo Pinto County, Texas. She was born on 11 Apr 1874 in Strawn, Texas. She died on 18 Feb 1950 in Temple, Bell County, Texas.

More About Isaac Mansfield Edwards:
Burial: 19 Mar 1945 in Mount Marion Cemetery, Strawn,
Texas Cause Of Death: Coronary Thrombosis and Embolism
Occupation: 1900 in Palo Pinto County, Texas; Farmer
Occupation: 1910 in Strawn, Texas; Carpenter
Occupation: 1920 in Weatherford, Texas; Carpenter
Occupation: 1930 in Strawn, Texas; Painter
Occupation: 1940 in Strawn, Texas; Painter

Notes for Isaac Mansfield Edwards:
Death certificate gives date of birth as February 1, 1868. 1900 U.S. census gives date of birth as February 1868. Headstone gives date of birth as February 1, 1870.

More About Mary Sophronia (Onie) Strawn:
Burial: 18 Feb 1950 in Mount Marion Cemetery, Strawn,
Texas Cause Of Death: Obstructive Jaundice

Notes for Mary Sophronia (Onie) Strawn:
Death certificate gives date of birth as April 11, 1874. 1900 U.S. census gives date of birth as April 1874. Headstone gives date of birth as April 11, 1875.

ii. Walter White Edwards, son of Ambrose Newton Edwards and Joanna Columbia Ardis was born on 31 Oct 1870 in Sulphur Springs, Texas. He died on 27 Nov 1938 in El Paso, Texas. He married Mary Anna King, daughter of Porter King and Eudorah Martha Bush in 1897 in Palo Pinto County, Texas. She was born on 23 Jul 1864 in Texas. She died on 23 Dec 1956 in Amarillo, Potter County, Texas.

More About Walter White Edwards:
Burial: 29 Nov 1938 in Evergreen Cemetery, El Paso,
Texas Cause Of Death: Cardiac Failure, Hypertension
Occupation: 1910; Gold Miner, Gorden, Palo Pinto County,
Texas
Occupation: 1920 ; Salesman, El Paso, Texas
Occupation: 1930 ; Geologist, El Paso, Texas

Notes for Walter White
   Edwards: Dear Mr. Edwards:
   Your request to our Geological Information Center for information on the Baking Powder mine was forwarded to me. Probably fewer than a half-dozen living people in all the southwest have even heard of
this property as it is one of the more obscure such in all New Mexico. I am not

aware that the property was ever examined by a trained geologist or engineer (unless your Edwards relatives were such and there is no known surviving record of their work). My extensive mines and prospects files are absolutely silent in regard to the Baking Powder. Nevertheless I have noted one or two very obscure references in my research.

The Baking Powder is located in the Rosedale Mining District at the extreme north end of the San Mateo mountains in southern Socorro county, New Mexico. I have not examined the mining claim records in the local courthouse for exact dates (mainly because you are the very first individual to ever request information on the property!) but would predict the claim (or claims) was located during latter part of the 19th century -- poss. mid-1890s -- as a result of the success of the well-known Rosedale mine and discovery of the nearby White Cap.

The "veins" in the Rosedale district are actually brecciated shear zones in the volcanic (rhyolitic) rocks The brecciated and sheared rhyolite has been recemented with a hard, bluish-white quartz and later with a clearer vein-type quartz. The entire vein mass is highly silicified and in those areas yielding the best gold values are heavily stained with the black and red oxides of manganese and iron respectively. Gold occurred in the native state in the upper oxidized portions of the vein but is very nearly absent in the sulfide portion at or below the water table. Remarkably, little or no silver is present. I would predict the Baking Powder "vein" to be similar in character to the above. Dr. Charles Ferguson's doctoral dissertation covered a large area extending from the southern end of the Rosedale District to the north well beyond White Cap and Big Rosa canyons. I asked Charlie if he knew the locality of the Baking Powder and other prospects and he indicated approximate locations for two unnamed mine workings about two miles north and northwest of the Rosedale which I feel are the White Cap and the Baking Powder. The projected location for the latter is approx. Sec3, T6S, R6W near the head of Big Rosa canyon.

Soon after the turn of the century, development on the Baking Powder had apparently progressed to the mining stage. According to a note in the Engineering and Mining Journal, 24 December 1903, p 988, the Baking Powder mine was said to be initiating "full operations," whatever that meant; Walter Edwards, undoubtedly your ancestor, was the manager. Unfortunately the operation failed to live up to expectations and within four years was facing foreclosure for $1200 in back wages (Soccoro Chieftan, 30 November 1907). The obvious conclusion is that the mine failed to develop pay ore in sufficient quantities to sustain the operation and it failed. And that is the current extent of the "historic" record!

I and my colleagues attempted to visit this prospect in May 2000, but despite our "approximate" location on the topo sheet, and a full day's search, four-wheeling, etc., we failed to locate it. I should note that the 'road' up Big Rosa canyon is, in places, a figment of the imagination -- we could have easily missed a small prospect off in the ponderosas! The Mount Whithington jeep road may pass within a mile of the mine on the west and that is the route I will next attempt.

Now that you have made a request for information, I shall keep a sharp lookout for additional data. I must yet peruse the pages of the few issues of the San Marcial Bee that have survived the ravages of time and will keep you in mind should anything materialize. Additionally I will examine the claim location records upon my next visit to the courthouse. On the other hand, I'd be most pleased to add to our archival files any information you'd be willing to share with us from your family's papers. Regards,

Robert W. Eveleth Senior
Mining Engineer Curator,
Mining Archives

Dear Mr. Edwards:

Recent research on several articles of local mining interest has, once again, led me through the pages of the Socorro Chieftain. Recalling your interest in the above, I made a copy of an article on the Baking Powder/Edwards Bros., reproduced below in its entirety:

Socorro Chieftain, 6/14/1902, p 4: "Rosedale, N. M., June 10m, 1902 -- Editor Chieftain -- Rosedale is quiet at present. Big Rosa, 2-1/2 miles to the northwest, shows great and rapidly increasing activity. Fully $5,000 worth of work is now underway and other contracts are being let. The immediate cause of this work was the discovery and partial development of the Baking Powder property of the Edwards Brothers of El Paso, Tex. This claim showed well from the surface but now at a depth of 55 feet it is exciting old time prospectors and tenderfeet alike by yielding a strong vein of high grade ore while picked samples show as high as 84 ounces in gold. Two or more stamp mills, stores, drink emporiums, a post office, dozens of cabins and tents, a good graded road up Big Rosa, and a couple of hundred men tearing into its mountain sides may be a vision, but as a miner and prospector of long experience I think this and more will be a reality within 12 months. Big Rosa may not be as good a mining camp as Cripple Creek, Colo. It may be better. The writer has no interest there and is not puffing the camp to "induce capital," but is sincere in saying that right now is a suitable and very favorable time to investigate Big Rosa.
There can be no harm in keeping an eye on the indicator." Signed: A. L. Heister."

As I continue to go through the pages of the Socorro Chieftan, I'll be sure to let you know if the writer's dream materialized.

Best Regards,
Robert W. Eveleth
Senior Mining Engineer

More About Mary Anna King:
Burial: 26 Dec 1956 in Llano Cemetery, Amarillo, Randall County, Texas
Living In: 1930 With her sister, Frances, in Amarillo, Potter County, Texas
Living In: 1935 El Paso, El Paso County, Texas
Living In: 1940 With her sister, Frances, in Amarillo, Potter County, Texas

Notes for Mary Anna King:
Death certificate and headstone give year of birth as 1861. Census records indicate year of birth is 1864.

See obituary of John Porter King.

1870 and 1880 U.S. census has her name as "Mollie".
----

iii.   Ambrose Edwin Edwards, son of Ambrose Newton Edwards and Joanna Columbia Ardis was born on 20 Mar 1872 in Sulphur Springs, Texas. He died on 15 Feb 1963 in Dallas, Texas. He married Anne Buntin Yarbrough, daughter of George Yarbrough and Margaret Augusta Herrin on 03 Jul 1901 in Grayson County, Texas. She was born on 15 Oct 1871 in Tyler, Texas. She died on 24 Oct 1955 in Dallas, Texas.

More About Ambrose Edwin Edwards:
Burial: 18 Feb 1963 in Restland Cemetery, Dallas,
Texas Cause Of Death: Cerebral Arteriosclerosis

Occupation: 1910 in Greenville, Texas; Real Estate Agent
Occupation: 1920 in Greenville, Texas; Real Estate Agent
Occupation: 1930 in Greenville, Texas; Farm Loan Agent
Occupation: 1940 in Dallas, Texas; Real Estate Proprietor

Notes for Ambrose Edwin Edwards:
Middle name of Edwin is probably after Doctor Edwin P. Becton of Sulphur
Springs, Texas.

 Birth date is from Social Security death index. Headstone has 1871 for year of birth
but this would conflict with the birth date of his brother, Walter White Edwards.

More About Anne Buntin Yarbrough:
Burial: 25 Oct 1955 in Restland Cemetery, Dallas,
Texas Cause Of Death: Coronary Occlusion

iv.   Marvin M. Edwards, son of Ambrose Newton Edwards and Joanna Columbia
Ardis was born on 28 Nov 1875 in Riley Springs, Texas. He died on 11 Sep 1900
in Strawn, Texas.

More About Marvin M. Edwards:
Burial: Mount Marion Cemetery, Strawn, Texas
Cause Of Death: Consumption (Tuberculosis)
Living In: 1900 in Palo Pinto County, Texas with his parents

v.   McDonald Edwards, son of Ambrose Newton Edwards and Joanna Columbia Ardis
was born on 10 Dec 1877 in Strawn, Texas. He died on 08 Nov 1957 in Lubbock,
Texas. He married Sally May Marchbanks, daughter of Finley W. Marchbanks and
Sarah A. Hix on 26 Feb 1899 in Strawn, Texas. She was born on 12 Feb 1877 in
Cleburne, Texas. She died on 27 Oct 1957 in Fort Worth, Texas.

More About McDonald Edwards:
Burial: 08 Nov 1957 in O'Donnell Cemetery, O'Donnell,
Texas Cause Of Death: Nephrosclerosis
Occupation: 1900 in Palo Pinto County, Texas; Hack Man
Occupation: 1910 in Palo Pinto County, Texas; Lumber Merchant
Occupation: 1920 in Palo Pinto County, Texas; Lumber Merchant
Occupation: 1930 in O'Donnell, Texas; Lumber Yard Manager
Occupation: 1940 in O'Donnell, Texas; Lumber Yard Proprietor

More About Sally May Marchbanks:
Burial: 28 Oct 1957 in O'Donnell Cemetery, O'Donnell,
Texas Cause Of Death: Chronic Myocarditis

Notes for Sally May Marchbanks:
Headstone gives name as Sallie May instead of Sally May.

vi. LeRoy Ardis Edwards, son of Ambrose Newton Edwards and Joanna Columbia Ardis was born on 27 Feb 1881 in Sulphur Springs, Texas. He died on 05 Dec 1951 in Loraine, Texas. He married Emma Georgie Irene Garland, daughter of Edward Warren Garland and Julia Rebecca Kimbell on 27 Jul 1921 in Roscoe, Texas. She was born on 23 Mar 1880 in Annona, Texas. She died on 17 Dec 1969 in Kerrville, Texas. He married Ada May Loflin, daughter of Daniel Vance Loflin and Margarite Sophia Crawley on 21 Nov 1906 in Palo Pinto County, Texas. She was born on 26 Apr 1886 in Palo Pinto County, Texas. She died on 15 Apr 1918 in Loraine, Texas.

vii. Becton Goodson Edwards, son of Ambrose Newton Edwards and Joanna Columbia Ardis was born on 29 Oct 1884 in Sulphur Springs, Texas. He died on 04 Dec 1960 in Dallas, Dallas County, Texas. He married Minnie Mae Strain, daughter of George Douglas Strain and Sarah Elizabeth Strawn on 04 Nov 1908 in Weatherford, Texas. She was born on 22 Feb 1887 in Strawn, Texas. She died on 28 Jul 1956 in Corsicana, Navarro County, Texas.

More About Becton Goodson Edwards:
Burial: 06 Dec 1960 in Grove Hill Cemetery, Dallas, Dallas County, Texas
Cause Of Death: Coronary Occlusion, Arteriosclerosis Heart Valve
Occupation: 1910 in Weatherford, Texas; Real Estate and Insurance Salesman
Occupation: 1920 in Forney, Texas; Postmaster
Occupation: 1930 in Forney, Texas; Pharmacist
Occupation: 1940 in Forney, Texas; Retail Drug Store Manager

Notes for Becton Goodson Edwards:
Named after Doctor Edwin P. Becton of Sulphur Springs, Texas. Doctor Becton served in the 22nd Texas Infantry, C.S.A., during the Civil War and is buried in Sulphur Springs City Cemetery, Sulphur Springs, Texas.

More About Minnie Mae Strain:
Burial: 28 Jul 1956 in Grove Hill Cemetery, Dallas, Dallas County, Texas Cause Of Death: Cerebral Hemorrhage

Notes for Minnie Mae Strain:
Death certificate has her middle name spelled "May". Headstone has her middle name spelled "Mae".

More About Becton Goodson Edwards and Minnie Mae Strain:
Marriage License: 03 Nov 1908 in Parker County, Texas
Marriage Fact: Married by George M. Oakley, Minister of the Gospel

viii. John McTyeire Edwards, son of Ambrose Newton Edwards and Joanna Columbia Ardis was born on 08 Dec 1888 in Eliasville, Texas. He died on 05 Oct 1970 in Killeen, Texas.

More About John McTyeire Edwards:
Burial: 09 Oct 1970 in Fort Sam Houston National Cemetery, San Antonio, Texas
Cause Of Death: Acute Myocardial Infarction, Generalized Arteriosclerosis

Living In: 1910 Greenville, Texas
Occupation: 1920 in Palo Pinto County, Texas; Bank Cashier
Occupation: 1930 in San Antonio, Texas; Hotel Clerk
Occupation: 1940 in San Antonio, Texas; Private Residence Gardener
Military Service: Bet. 19 Sep 1917-24 Mar 1919 ; Sergeant First Class, World War One

Notes for John McTyeire
Edwards: Never Married

Probably named after John McTyeire of Russell County, Alabama.

Served in HQ Company, 165th Depot Brigade, U.S. Army
----

10.   **Edward Warren Garland** was born on 28 Oct 1825 in Giles County, Tennessee. He died on 12 May 1897 in Texas. He married **Julia Rebecca Kimbell**.

11.   **Julia Rebecca Kimbell** was born on 31 Mar 1845 in Texas. She died on 26 Jan 1908 in Texas.

More About Edward Warren Garland:
Burial: Garland Cemetery, Red River County, Texas

More About Julia Rebecca Kimbell:
Burial: Garland Cemetery, Red River County, Texas

Julia Rebecca Kimbell and Edward Warren Garland had the following child:
5.   i. Emma Georgie Irene Garland, daughter of Edward Warren Garland and Julia Rebecca Kimbell was born on 23 Mar 1880 in Annona, Texas. She died on 17 Dec 1969 in Kerrville, Texas. She married LeRoy Ardis Edwards, son of Ambrose Newton Edwards and Joanna Columbia Ardis on 27 Jul 1921 in Roscoe, Texas. He was born on 27 Feb 1881 in Sulphur Springs, Texas. He died on 05 Dec 1951 in Loraine, Texas.

Generation 5

16.   **Ambrose Edwards**, son of William Newton Edwards and Mary Whatley was born on 16 Apr 1805 in Wilkes County, Georgia. He died on 06 Oct 1884 in Dale County, Alabama. He married **Emeline James Gaulding**, daughter of John Gaulding and Martha Gaulding in 1827 in South Carolina.

17.   **Emeline James Gaulding**, daughter of John Gaulding and Martha Gaulding was born on 10 Feb 1810 in Virginia. She died on 01 Jan 1886 in Dale County, Alabama.

More About Ambrose Edwards:
Burial: Pleasant Hill Methodist Cemetery, Ozark, Alabama
Living In: 1830 Talbot County, Georgia
Living In: 1840 Russell County, Alabama
Occupation: 1850 in Russell County, Alabama; Farmer
Occupation: 1860 in Dale County, Alabama; Farmer
Occupation: 1870 in Dale County, Alabama; Farmer
Occupation: 1880 in Dale County, Alabama; Farmer
Military Service: ; Matthews Company, Dale County Reserves, Dale County, Alabama C.S.A.
Property: 1850 in Russell County, Alabama; 150 Acres Improved and 252 Acres Unimproved
Property: 1860 in Dale County, Alabama; 260 Acres Improved and 260 Acres Unimproved
Property: 1870 in Dale County, Alabama; 1250 Acres Improved and 500 Acres Unimproved

Property: 1880 in Dale County, Alabama; 75 Acres Improved and 360 Acres Unimproved

Notes for Ambrose Edwards:
Originally buried in Pleasant Hill Cemetery near Westville, moved to new Pleasant Hill Cemetery near Ozark in 1942 when Fort Rucker was established
----
Moved to Talbot County, Georgia in 1829.
Moved to Russell County, Alabama in 1839. This part of Russell County is now in Lee County, Alabama
Moved to Dale County, Alabama near Westville in November 1854.

Obituary of Ambrose Edwards

Crittenden's Mill, Ala. December 7th 1884 (Published in the Southern Star, December 31, 1884)

Ambrose Edwards was born in Wilkes county Georgia, April 16th 1805 and died in Dale county Alabama, October the 6th 1884, in triumphs of the Christian faith. He was happily married to Emeline J. Gaulding October the 4th 1827 in Bibb county Georgia. In 1820 he moved to Talbot county Georgia and in 1839 he settled in Russell county Alabama where he joined the Methodist Episcopal Church and was Happily converted to God in which faith and communion he lived a consistent and devoted member to the date of his death. He was the father of eleven children five of whom have preceded him to the better land and the other six (all sons) are trying to follow in the footsteps of their father: one a minister of the gospel: four are superintendents of Sabbath schools and the other a church secretary.

No wife ever had a more devoted husband, no children a more affectionate father. His greatest ambition in life was to do good and to see his children good and honorable. Of the seven boys he raised to be men not a dram drinker nor a profane swearer was in the number. He was for many years a practical steward of the church till the mantle fell on his oldest son. He was a man of great will power but was always conservative in his intercourse with his fellow man. Few men were ever more instrumental in settling difficulties between brethren and neighbors than he.

While he was deprived of an early education his practical good sence always gave him first rank in the county where he lived. The last thirty years of his life was spent in Dale county. The writer was with him day and night the greater portion of his last sickness: and such patience he hardly ever witnessed. The only thing that seemed to trouble his mind was leaving his aged and devoted companion who had shared his joys and sorrows through a married life of fifty-seven years. What a happy reunion it will be when the companion who still lingers on the shore of time only waiting for the summons, and the children all meet if faithful around the throne of God.

More About Emeline James Gaulding:
Burial: Pleasant Hill Methodist Cemetery, Ozark, Alabama

Notes for Emeline James Gaulding:
Originally buried in Pleasant Hill Cemetery near Westville, moved to new Pleasant Hill Cemetery near Ozark in 1942 when Fort Rucker was established.
-- ----

Obituary of Emeline James Gaulding

Emeline J. Edwards, daughter of John Gaulding, was born in the state of Virginia in the month of February 1810. With her parents she removed to Hancock County Georgia in 1818. In that County she was converted at the age of eleven years and joined the Methodist E. Church, in which communion she lived sixty-four years without a stain upon her pure and spotless character. During the year 1827 she was married to Mr. Ambrose Edwards of Monroe County, Georgia. A few years after the happy event they removed to Alabama and settled in old Russell County. Although at the time of their marriage Mr. Edwards was not a member of any Church, not a professor in Jesus Christ, yet by her pure and sweet spirit he was so powerfully influenced in regard to salvation from sin and death as to become deeply concerned. At Salem, of old Russell County, 1839 he was converted and joined the Church of his Christian (.......?) In November 1854 they removed to Dale County and settled near Pleasant Hill Church and became members of that Church.

She was the mother of 11 children, 8 sons and 3 daughters, 5 of whom are dead and 6 living. All of those who lived to sufficient age joined the Church of their fond parents and are strong and devoted members of the Church. Such was the influence of the mother upon the whole family that they are perfectly united in affection, religion and cooperation. In this respect they constitute a model family. How ever distant from each other the children realize their unity in the mother. While breathing her last, a present was received, the gift of a son in Texas. As mother and grandmother she was an extraordinary woman. As wife she was all the Bible commands. As Church member and Christian she was perfect. To everybody she was tender, gentle and considerate. She always had a word of cheer and smile of appreciation for the toiling and struggling ones in righteousness. She heartily endorsed every enterprise of her Church and supported it's institution. Her Pastor always found her in sympathy with his efforts to build up the Church and save sinners. The writer has known her 30 years and knows no fault in her life. At 7 A. M. January 1, 1886 she ascended to glory. She died at the home of her son, C.A.B. Edwards, and was buried at Pleasant Hill on Saturday beside her husband, amid tears of sorrow and hope.

By Rev. Angus Dowling

Emeline James Gaulding and Ambrose Edwards had the following children:

    i.   Martha Louise Edwards, daughter of Ambrose Edwards and Emeline James Gaulding was born on 20 Jul 1828 in Georgia. She died on 09 Aug 1881 in Alabama. She married Hope Hull Mizell, son of William Mizell and Mary Love on 07 Dec 1843 in Russell County, Alabama. He was born on 20 Sep 1820 in Baldwin County, Georgia. He died on 02 Mar 1887 in Haw Ridge, Alabama.

More About Martha Louise Edwards:
b: 20 Jul 1848
Burial: Haw Ridge, Alabama

More About Hope Hull
Mizell:
Burial: Ebenezer Cemetery, Dale County, Alabama
Occupation: 1850 in Russell County, Alabama; Farmer
Occupation: 1860; Farmer, Dale County, Alabama
Occupation: 1870; Merchant, Coffee County, Alabama
Occupation: 1880; Merchant, Haw Ridge, Alabama
Military Service: Dale County, Alabama, Home Guard, C.S.A.
Property: 1860 in Dale County, Alabama; 60 Acres Improved and 260 Acres Unimproved

    ii.   LeRoy Marion Edwards, son of Ambrose Edwards and Emeline James Gaulding was born on 29 Aug 1830 in Talbot County, Georgia. He died on 24 May 1898 in Brundidge, Alabama. He married Martha Mizell, daughter of William Mizell and Mary Love on 06 Nov 1849 in Russell County, Alabama. She was born on 04 Feb 1829 in Houston County, Georgia. She died on 30 Oct 1908 in Brundidge, Pike County, Alabama.

More About LeRoy Marion Edwards:
Burial: Pleasant Hill Methodist Cemetery, Ozark, Alabama
Occupation: 1850 in Russell County, Alabama; Farmer
Occupation: Bet. 1860-1880 in Dale County, Alabama; Farmer,
Occupation: 1866 ; Justice of the Peace, Dale County, Alabama.
Commissioned July 6, 1866.
Occupation: 1891; Justice of the Peace, Dale County, Alabama. Appointed
January 29, 1891, Commisioned February 13, 1891.
Occupation: Bet. 1893-1895 in Served in Alabama State Legislature
Occupation: 1894 in Dale County, Alabama; County Superintendant of
Education. Elected August 6, 1894 and commisioned September 19, 1894.
Military Service: Bet. 26 Aug 1862-1865 ; Co. E, 53rd Alabama Mounted
Infantry, C.S.A.
Property: 1850 in Russell County, Alabama; 20 Acres Improved and 60
Acres Unimproved
Property: 1860 in Dale County, Alabama; 60 Acres Improved and 100
Acres Unimproved
Property: 1870 in Dale County, Alabama; 160 Acres Improved and 140
Acres Unimproved

Notes for LeRoy Marion Edwards:
    Promoted to the rank of the rank of Second Lieutenant in Company E, 53rd
Alabama Mounted Infantry on November 15, 1863. (Alabama Partisan Rangers).

    Enlisted August 26, 1862 and served until the end of the War.

    Served in Alabama State Legislature 1893-1895 Served
    as Justice of the Peace in Pike County, Alabama

    Died in the home of his daughter, Mary Love Edwards, while visiting her.

More About Martha Mizell:
Burial: Pleasant Hill Methodist Cemetery, Ozark, Alabama
Living In: 1900 Shellman, Randolph County, Georgia with her daughter Emeline
and her family.

Notes for Martha Mizell:
Headstone gives March 4, 1828 for birth date. 1900 U.S. census gives
February 1829 for birth. Headstone has October 30, 1908 for date of death.

More About LeRoy Marion Edwards and Martha Mizell:
Marriage License: 05 Nov 1849 in Russell County, Alabama
Marriage Fact: 06 Nov 1849 in Married by J. Scaife, Minister of the Gospel

iii.   John Wilson Gaulding Edwards, son of Ambrose Edwards and Emeline James
        Gaulding was born on 10 Jan 1833 in Talbot County, Georgia. He died about
        1858. He married Sarah Frances Sharp, daughter of Jehu Harrison Sharp and
        Tabitha Jane White on 04 Oct 1854 in Meriwether County, Georgia. She was
        born on 30 Oct 1836 in Georgia. She died on 09 Jul 1904 in Texas.

More About Sarah Frances Sharp:
Burial: Rutland Cemetery, Douglassville, Cass County, Texas

More About John Wilson Gaulding Edwards and Sarah Frances
Sharp: Marriage Fact: Married by John L. Williams, M.G.

iv.   William Archibald Edwards, son of Ambrose Edwards and Emeline James Gaulding
was born on 28 Feb 1835 in Talbot County, Georgia. He died on 12 Dec 1926 in
Dallas, Texas. He married Eliza Jones White, daughter of Theophilus White and Mary
H. Jett on 05 Jan 1858 in Russell County, Alabama. She was born on 08 Apr 1836 in
Meriwether County, Georgia. She died on 06 Sep 1922 in Dallas, Texas.

More About William Archibald Edwards:
Burial: 14 Dec 1926 in Oak Cliff Cemetery,Dallas,Texas
Occupation: 1861; Farmer
Occupation: 1870 in Autauga County, Alabama; Minister
Occupation: 1880 in Farmersville, Texas; School Teacher
Occupation: 1900 in Eagle Ford, Dallas County, Texas; Minister
Occupation: 1910 in Dallas, Dallas County, Texas; Retired
Occupation: 1920 in Dallas, Dallas County, Texas; Retired - Living with his
daughter Eliza and her husband George Cochran
Occupation: ; Methodist Minister
Military Service: Bet. 03 Jul 1861-13 Aug 1863; Company E, 15th
Alabama Infantry, C.S.A.

Notes for William Archibald Edwards:

Published in:
Southern Star, Jan. 5, 1916

Dallas, Tex., Nov. 11, 1915.

Dear Ruf:
   I wrote you for a list of my dear old Co. E. 15th Alabama Regiment who are now
living, and as you were sick Bro. Charley Edwards sent me the following list vis.-
W.R. Painter, W.C. Mizell Ozark; J.R. Edwards, Mat Williams, Ariton; C. V.
Atkinson, Newton; Newt Curenton, Haw Ridge; Albert Austin, Daleville; W.D.
Byrd, B.W. Fleming, Enterprise; Dorse Fleming, Geneva; C.G. Dillard, Ozark
Route 1. To this I add the Texas list---Capt. Wm. A. Edwards, 4019 Bowser St.
Dallas Texas; A.N. Edwards, Gordon, Tex.;Y.M. Edwards, Alvin, Tex.; J.P. Martin,
Italy, Tex.; Ben Martin, Waxahachie, Tex.; Wm. Mobly Crandal, Dallas County,
Tex. The above constitute the list of survivors as I have it. If you know of any
others please add them to this.
   The Company left home with 84 men enlisted all told 200. Returned home
after surrender 100. So you see 100 brave and as good men as Dale or any
other county ever raised sleep in some Northern or Southern cemetery or in
shallow crude graves on some battle field, or possibly some were buried
under the winter snow or to decay on some bloody hard fought battle ground and
their bones to bleach under a burning sun, and to their dust and memory we say
farewell dear comrades, and we hope some day to meet you beyond the flash
and roar of artillery and rattle of musketry.
   It will probably be some interest to the friends and survivors of Co. E. to read a
short write up of the Company which I hope you will have the Star to publish and

send a copy to all living members. I t will likely be the last message they will ever get from me as I am now past eighty and they are not in their teens. I want each to take this as a personal letter and I would be glad to have a letter from all of them.

No better Co. of citizens soldiers ever left any community than left Westville on the 18th day of July 1861, 54 years ago the past July. No more sumptuous feast was ever spread for departing patriots than was spread under the shade of the beautiful oaks that stood around old Darian church. The loving hands that prepared it have long since been wafted beyond the curse of war and rage of battles by the angels of God. In all my life I have never seen deeper and purer emotions or heard so tender farewells as followed that sumptuous feast. Husbands and wives embraced in tender love and with many it was the last embrace---fathers kissed their only babes---mothers threw a mothers arm around her son and with a mothers deep prayer sent her soldier boy to the conflict of battle and perils of war. And some of the boys felt the tender touch of the bride-to-be as they clasped hands that day. It thrilled their souls and nerved their arm for deeds of daring until they either perished in the campaign or returned home under the furled banner of the stars and bars. I have often been anxious to know if any of them that got back got left. "That day many parted, Where few shall meet."

That night we camped at Fraziers mill on Pea river and almost the entire company took a bath, and if there were either snakes, alligators or varmints for miles around they took to the hills and swamps never to return. Such a babel of voices and splashing of water I have never heard. The next night we camped in the open streets of Perote, and its bests families welcomed us with royal favors, and our third night out we stopped at Union Springs and spent the Sabbath there, which stay will always be kindly remembered by Co.E. That was the day of the first Manassas battle and Bull Run episode. Many thought the war was ended and some kind hearted mothers hoped their boys might see Richmond before they were disbanded. Well the boys saw Richmond and beyond. How little we knew of war and the bitter cup before the south.

We next find ourselves organized as Co. E. in the 15th Alabama Regiment. Nothing of special interest to the Co. E until our regiment camped at Camp Toombs between Centerville and Manassas. There Dick Neil died. This is worthy of mentioning because he was the first member of Co. E that died and the first one that had died in a regimental camp. He was honored as but few soldiers are ever honored. The Regiment was drawn up to witness the solemn burial, and Co. E with reversed arms and muffled drum followed the corpse to the road that leads from Centerville to Manassas; and there in plain coffin with a soldiers blanket for a winding sheet we buried him and a platoon of Co. E fired a soldier salute about the lonely grave, and there on the lonely spot unmarked by human hands and unknown to the busy world that passes that way to-day sleeps the dust of Corporal Neil without a stain on his name or character at home or in the army. It was the first crude shock that came to Co. E and it threw a gloom over the folks at home as nothing had done. All began to realize that war was on, and I remember at that camp Col. Canty told me it would be a terrible struggle. We spent the winter at Manassas and the only thing of special interest to Co. E was the task of getting boards for winter quarters, a task I never heard a single member complain of.

I was sent with my Company across Bull Run to the east of Centerville in the hilly and wooded country that had been but little occupied by soldiers up to that time, to get boards to cover huts for winter quarters. And old federal sympathizer lived about half a mile from our camp and killed hogs one day, it would have been better had he killed all he had. I went up to his house and wanted to buy a hasslet. He asked 50 cents for it and at that time we thought ten or fifteen cents good pay. I went back where the boys were at work and related what had occurred and I saw one of them give a significant wink and asked "Do you love hasslet Captain and I told him yes." Well to make a long story short, next morning when I woke up there was a ham of a 250 pound hog slipped under my tent and a large hasslet hanging in front and

John Trawick, my cook, singing, whistling and frying liver and ham just as happy as he could get and you remember John could get very happy. I ate it and asked no questions for conscience sake, and as well as I remember it was the first and last stolen meat I ate during the war.

1862 was the fighting year of the war. Before the ground had thawed and the buds had burst into leaves we were taken from our pleasant quarters and transferred to the valley and received a formal introduction to Stonewall Jackson. There are two incidents in this campaign I wish to relate, not battles the historian does that, but unnoticed and unknown to the historian yet of interest to the Co. E. I allude to the death of Jno. Trawick and Lieut. Mills. John Trawick was killed almost under the guns of Harper Ferry, when we halted in our pursuit of Banks. We were resting on the turn-pike when a gun accidentally discharged and shattered poor Johns heel to pieces. He was carried to a Winchester Hospital, and in a few days I received notice he was dead.

I want to say this for John Trawick, I detailed him to cook for me, and he did more for my comfort than any one else has ever done. He carried my luggage on marches. (He was big and strong.) When the Regiment halted if it was mid-night. He spread my bedding and cooked my supper no matter how tired he was, and I have often wondered if Israels chariot was sent down to take that rough, rugged yet noble son of nature to a bright and better world.

Lieut. Mills was killed at Cross Keys, when an unexpected retreat was ordered our regiment. He was a hightoned, brave Christian gentlemen confided in at home and honored and loved in the army. He was devoted to his mess and his mess to him quiet, intelligent, refined and dignified a high type of a Christian gentleman yet he always impressed me that a cloud was over his spirits an I have never thought he expected to survive the war, and I thought and still think that terrible specter of presentment was ever before his eyes.

At night after the terrible battle of Gains Mills at Richmond after night fall had covered the field of carnage and death which was strewed with dead and dying, I fell on Billy Robinson, a fine specimen of manhood, tall, angular swarthy, hair as black as a crow and fearless as a lion. He told me he was mortally wounded and could live but a little while. He asked me who held the field I told him we held it. Then he said I am willing to die. Tell father I died fighting for my home and country, that I died brave and I feel I am prepared for a better world. His father was a Methodist preacher.

Co. E did the fighting for Hood's division at Suffolk. It held the line against great odds early morning till night, did the picket duty till mid night and covered the retreat of the army twenty or twenty five to Black Water River. I doubt if any Company ever withstood so strong and persistent attack, more courageously and firmly than did Co. E. A whole brigade against one company for an entire day, but we had the position on them.

During the engagement I met Jess Flowers, hat off sleeves rolled up, and sweat rolling from his brow. He said Captain they have killed my mess mate Cameron, and I am ready to fight the whole Yankee army. I believe Jess would have tried it. Cameron was a good man and soldier and died with his face to the enemy. The only three men I detailed to cook for me were Trawick, Flowers and Charley Jones; the two first were killed and Charley Jones crippled for life.

While we were at Suffolk, the battle of the wilderness was fought andfighting Joe Hooper whipped. Thence we followed Lee to Gettysburg, which with the surrender of Fort Donaldson sealed the fate of the Confederacy. They first brought Grant, the man of destiny into the lime light, and second, settled the question of invasion, and so reduced Lee's army that it was only a question of time when it would succumb to superior force. But I wish to say a few things about that great and fatal battle. First the 15th,
Alabama went further in that battle than any other troop, second Co. E went as far as any part of the Regiment and staid as long. The men fired their guns until the barrel become so hot they could not hold and load them.

The death of private Holloway was to me the sadest feature of thissanguinary struggle. We were well protected behind a great rock about 4 feet high, the enemy equally protected behind a rock fence not more than 50 yards in front of us, and Captain Park reported a flanking division (Sickles) coming in our rear. Col. Oats ordered a charge and mounted the rock himself and discharged the contents of a six shooter in the face of the enemy. No one would follow but Holloway who mounted the roch [rock], fell on his left knee, fixed his musket and a ball from the enemy crashed through his left temple and he fell dead on the feet of his gallant Colonel. How gallant! How useless! I saw the gallant deed and in the rage of battle and reign of death I thought what a sorrow it would carry to the bereaved wife and ten orphaned children far away in our beloved Alabama.

But our hearts were not always heavy and our heads bowed with grief. The soldier out of battle was ready for favor and the evening before the Gettysburg battle Co. E. was out on picket line.

Gen. Lee had ordered no private property disturbed and among the grove of large oaks in which [we] were camped a bunch of fine hogs had been browsing for acorns all day. Co. E's mouth had been watering all day for a taste of Yankee pork. Late that evening the Colonel told me there would be rations that evening and to let any one kill one of those hogs. I called the Co. together and told them to kill one of the biggest hogs and before I could stop then they had killed three and had a fourth so nearly dead I allowed them to finish it. But a very amazing thing occurred during the hog killing. I had two men in my Company, some of you may still remember them for no Company could well be without two such men. One was Sam Hog a great big over grown man, and Peters a small little fellow, and I looked out and saw Peters coming towards me closely pursued by Hog, nearly in touching distance and at every leap he would cry "help me Captain! Help me Captain." I called a halt-inquired the trouble, Hog said Peters hit him with a rock and nearly broke his leg, and Peters gasping for breath said "Captain you told us to kill the biggest hog we could find and he was the biggest one I saw. It was so ludicrous Hog burst into loud laughter and limping turned to his quarters. The truth was Peters had missed his mark.

One more incident that was very amusing to me, and the strange part is it never cease to be amusing to me. The parties to this incident were uncle Dave Snell and Latimer, both as true and worth men as ever girded their shoes with the accentments of war or shouldered a musket, both are now under the soil beyond the din of battle.

One morning at roll call Latimer came up with a broken arm and it was broken after the rest of the Company had gone to bed, Uncle Dave was to report the case and with the usual gravity of old men. He said he and Latimer went to the spring to get water to cook and coming up from the spring with a bucket of water his foot slipped, he fell and broke his arm. No one dared question Uncle Dave's word, but it seemed strange to me they should be out at midnight after water to cook, I said nothing knowing full well if it had any rich or racy features the boys could not keep it from me. So I pretty soon got a full statement of the case, and not very much like Uncle Daves. They had gone to a nearby apple orchard and Latimer climbed a tree and sized a hornets nest and in his hasty retreat a limb broke, he fell and broke his arm. A few days after on the march I asked the old soldier to tell me exactly how the accident occurred and with great precision he related the affair to where Latimer started up the hill with his camp kettle of water and said "Captain he got slickest fall I ever saw." Well says I, Uncle Dave were there any hornets about the spring. "Captain he said I'll tell you all about it. I told him no I knew it all. I never blamed him not Latimer only for not knowing the difference between an apple and a hornet nest. In fact I never blamed Adam so much for eating that red apple Eve gave him, I expect I would have done as he did. This occurred as well as I remember at Raccoon ford of the Rapidam.

In conclusion of this article to my old true and tried friends and comrades-friends and soldiers tried in the concible [crucible?] of fire. There are a few things I reflect on with great pleasure.

1st, after the surrender Co. E returned from the scenes of battle and war, with true manhood and moral character and honest purpose entered honorable business and have been successful and useful citizens.

2nd, that my original mess eight of us are still living and constitute nearly half of the now living members of the Company.

3rd, and last and by far the most pleasing reflection is that I treated my Company as gentlemen, They were gentlemen at home and I could see no reason why they should not be treated as gentlemen in the army and I do not remember having punished one of my men, I consciously believed discipline could be maintained without it, and I do not believe the Confederacy ever produced a better Company on the march a more orderly one in camps, nor a braver one in battle, and soon the last of us will hear the tatoo for final sleep and rest, and the revile. When the trumpet of God shall awake and the sleeping dust of earths millions, and may we answer the roll call on that side of the river that makes glad the city of God.

Wm. A. EDWARDS

First Lieutenant July 3, 1861; Captain March 6, 1862; Resigned September 2, 1863 and served as Chaplain for the duration of the War.

Enlisted on July 3, 1861 at Fort Mitchell, Alabama and served until resigning to become Chaplain on September 2, 1863.

Engagements: Winchester, Cross Keys, Cold Harbor, Fredricksburg, Suffolk, Hazel River, 2nd Manassas, Chantilly, Harpers Ferry, Sharpsburg, Shepardstown, Gettysburg, Battle Mount.

Pre War residence was Westville, Alabama.

June 3-August 1, 1863 -- The Gettysburg Campaign..- Report of Col. William C. Oates, Fifteenth Alabama Infantry.

AUGUST 8,1863.

SIR: I have the honor to report, in obedience to orders from brigade headquarters, the participation of my regiment in the battle near Gettysburg on the 2d ultimo. My regiment occupied the center of the brigade when the line of battle was formed. During the advance, the two regiments on my right were moved by the left flank across my rear, which threw me on the extreme right of the whole line. I encountered the enemy's sharpshooters posted behind a stone fence, and sustained some loss thereby. It was here that Lieut. Col. Isaac B. Feagin, a most excellent and gallant officer, received a severe wound in the right knee, which caused him to lose his leg. Privates (A.) Kennedy, of Company B, and (William) Trimner, of Company G, were killed at this point, and Private (G. E.) Spencer, Company D, severely wounded. After crossing the fence, I received an order from Brigadier-General Law to left-wheel my regiment and move in the direction of the heights upon my left, which order I failed to obey, for the reason that when I received it I was rapidly advancing up the mountain, and in my front I discovered a heavy force of the enemy. Besides this, there was great difficulty in accomplishing the maneuver at that moment, as the regiment on my left (Forty-seventh Alabama) was crowding me on the left, and running into my regiment, which had already created considerable confusion. In the event that I had obeyed the order, I should have come in contact with the regiment on my left, and also have exposed my right flank to an enfilading fire from the enemy. I therefore continued to press forward, my right passing over the top of the mountain, on the right of the line. On reaching the foot of the mountain below, I found the enemy in heavy force, posted in rear of large rocks upon a slight elevation beyond a depression of some 300 yards in width between the base of the mountain and the open plain beyond. I engaged them, my right meeting the left of their line exactly. Here I lost several gallant officers and men. After firing two or three rounds, I discovered that the enemy were giving way in my front. I ordered a charge, and the enemy in my front fled, but that portion of his line confronting the two companies on my left held their ground, and continued a most galling fire upon my left. Just at this moment, I discovered the regiment on my left (Forty-seventh Alabama) retiring. I halted my regiment as its left reached a very large rock, and ordered a left-wheel of the regiment, which was executed in good order under fire, thus taking advantage of a ledge of rocks running off in a line perpendicular to the one I had just abandoned, and affording very good protection to my men. This position enabled me to keep up a constant flank and cross fire upon the enemy, which in less than five minutes caused him to change front. Receiving reinforcements, he charged me five times, and was as often repulsed with heavy loss. Finally, I discovered that the enemy had flanked me on the right, and two regiments were moving rapidly upon my rear and not 200 yards distant, when, to save my regiment from capture or destruction, I ordered a retreat. Having become exhausted from fatigue and the excessive heat of the day, I turned the command of the regiment over to Capt. B. A. Hill, and instructed him to take the men off the field, and reform the regiment and report to the brigade.

My loss was, as near as can now be ascertained, as follows, to wit: 17 killed upon the field, 54 wounded and brought off the field, and 90 missing, most of whom are either killed or wounded. Among the killed and wounded are 8 officers, most of whom were very gallant and efficient men.

Recapitulation.--Killed, 17; wounded, 54; missing, 90; total, 161.

I am, lieutenant, most respectfully, your obedient servant,

W. C. OATES,
Colonel, Commanding Fifteenth Alabama Regiment

Lieut. B.O. PETERSON,
Acting Assistant Adjutant-General

See "NOTES" for Eliza Jones White for William Archibald Edwards autobiography.

More About Eliza Jones White:
died: 06 Sep 1922 in Dallas,
Texas
Burial: 08 Sep 1922 in Oak Cliff Cemetery, Dallas, Texas

Notes for Eliza Jones White:
Oak Cliff Cemetery records give first name as "Elvira".

Autobiography Or some incidents in my life
                    by Reverend William A.Edwards
(husband of Eliza Jones White)

I was born in Talbot County, Georgia on the 28th day of February, 1835. The day is designated in history as the cold Friday. It was the coldest day in the history of that country up to that date and I am sure that it has never been equaled since. It was said that the freeze was so powerful and deep that great trees of the forest burst and many of them died.

My father's name was Ambrose Edwards. He lived to be eighty-two years of age. My grandfather's name was William Edwards. He died at the age of eighty-four. I think he was born in the eastern part of Virginia and my impression is that he was the son of Ambrose Edwards.

My grandmother Edwards was Mary Whatley. I know very little of her family. I never saw any near kin on my grandmother's side of the house.

My father had a house built on his farm to take care of his parents in their old age. They had not occupied it more than a month before my grandmother died and grandfather then lived with his children, making his home with his youngest son, William Edwards.

My grandfather made a profession of religion and received the sacrament on his deathbed.

My father, Ambrose Edwards, joined the Methodist Church at the age of twenty-five years and was one of the best men I ever knew.

My mother was Emeline James Gaulding, the daughter of John Gaulding. She died at the age of seventy-six. My grandfather Gaulding died of yellow fever in Mobile, Alabama when about sixty years old.

I never knew my grandmother Gaulding's maiden name or Christian name. I remember very distinctly seeing my father returning from the post office handing my mother a letter notifying her of the death of her father and the deep grief it produced on her refined and emotional nature. Mother died in the seventy-seventh year and both were buried in Westville, Dale County, Alabama.

My Edwards ancestors were robust in mind and body; were not afraid of anything; they nearly all acquired good property, but none of my father's family took much to books. On the other hand, my mother was a cultivated woman, about as much so as any raised in her day. The Gaulding family was cultivated and intelligent. Archibald Gaulding, the uncle for whom "A" in my name stands, was one of Georgia's most intelligent citizens. He was the most fascinating gentleman I nearly ever knew, as neat as a pin, as handsome as Absalom, as polite as Chesterfield, thoroughly educated, he was a man of mark. He served his state in the legislature, was a candidate for governor, but defeated, was for two terms auditor of the state road, and for many years, the State Masonic Lecturer and considered the brightest mason in the state.

I received my strong bodily constitution from the Edwards side and whatever taste or acquirements I may have in literature comes from my mother's family. I believe that my general knowledge exceeds that of any of my Edwards kin with whom I have met.

At the age of 14 I professed religion at Shady Grove Church in Lee County, Alabama. With my conversion came a clear call to the ministry, neither of which I have ever since doubted.

On the morning of the 5th day of January, 1858 I married Eliza Jones Mizell, the widow of James S. Mizell, and daughter of Theophilus White. We have raised eight children to be grown, two boys and six girls, all of them married. We have 27 grandchildren, six of which died, and as we grow older our life becomes more unified and happy. The names of our children are, respectfully: Theophilus Ambrose Edwards
Mary James Cora (Mrs. J. A. Skillern)
Annie Lee (Mrs. S. N. Neathery) Willie
Maud (Mrs. T. B. Lester) Mattie
Elizabeth (Mrs. B. L. Jones) Carrie
Louise (Mrs. J. L. Wilson)

Eliza (Lida) Emeline (Mrs. Geo. B.
Cochran) William Archibald Edwards, Jr.
There were no events in my childhood of unusual interest, I was considered forward,
egotistical, and full of pranks and mischief, and a superabundance of life. I cared
little for books until my conversion and union with the church. From that
day until the present books have been my best and most constant companion.

It seems to me now I must have been a boy of unusual endurance. I used to
pick cotton all day and then hunt possums and coons with father's Negroes nearly
all night. The first money I ever had was twenty-five cents and I paid it all for a
money purse and then wore the purse out carrying it in my pocket and never had
a cent to put in it. I next made fifty cents and bought a pistol with that and one day
all left home but me and I spent the entire day shooting chickens and never hit
one. I then swapped the pistol for an old vest and mother wouldn't let me wear it.
That ended the speculation.

I felt the call to the ministry from the day of my conversion and I suppose I have
made some of what the world would call sacrifices to preach. My uncle, for whom I
was named, offered to give me a legal profession if I would accept it, but I felt I
must preach. When I entered the ministry I was offered a law partnership with a
guarantee of $2.500.00 for the first year with every prospect of a large increase
and yet I declined it to enter the ministry and I am now at the age of sixty-two more
than pleased with my choice. The lawyer that made the offer was in one of two
years killed by a stroke of lightning and had I accepted the offer, some ill fatality
might have befallen me ere this.

I supposed my war record will interest my family more than my ministry as
the family is familiar with the latter.

Early in the summer of sixty I raised a company of volunteers, went to the war as its
first lieutenant and was soon promoted to captain in which capacity I served until near
the close of the war and received the appointment of missionary to the soldiers,
resigned and came home. The immediate cause of my resignation was the promotion
of Major Lowther to the Colonelcy, a man I had refused to serve under.

We left home for Virginia the 21st day of June. The day after the Battle of Bull
Run was fought; we rendezvoused at the Ft. Mitchell near Columbus, Georgia and
was organized in the 15th Alabama regiment as Company "E" and when we
reached Virginia was placed in Trumble's Brigade, Ewell's Division, Army of
Northern Virginia. Law afterward commanded the brigade and General J. B. Hood
the division. We were under General Jackson in all of his valley campaigns and
cooperated with Lee against McClellan in the seven days fight around Richmond.
General Jackson's forces came from the Valley and struck to the rear of the
Federal Army at Mechanicsville, six miles north of Richmond. In this battle
General Ewell, I think, saved Lee's army from being routed by his presence and
bravery. The confederates had almost fallen into a panic when the brave old man,
with hat in hand, headed the retreating men crying at the top of his voice:
"Men for God's sake, fight. You must fight, you must fight."

His presence and cheering words acted like magic. His men rallied a well nigh lost
battle. I have never seen this stated in history, yet I always thought this saved the day.
There were some incidents of this battle too pathetic not to mention. We slept that
night on the battlefield, among the dead and dying. In wandering about in the dark to
look for my men I stumbled on a dead man and by some strange impulse I stooped,
passed my hand over his face and recognized him to be Andrew Wilson, a young man
who had boarded at my father's and taught school. I called for a light, searched his
person and found on him a fine gold watch, $2.00 in silver, which I sent home to his
parents. I also found a cousin, his name was Carlisle, a noble youth and I always
thought one of the most handsome men I ever saw. A minie ball had entered his left
lung. He was sitting up with his head bowed forward and ever and anon, the gurgling
sound told the sad tale that life was rapidly passing away. He was suffering intensely. I
asked him if he knew me. He said "It's Cousin Billie". I asked him if I could help him
and he muttered rather indistinctly "water". I took a canteen of water from a dead man
and I held it to his mouth and he drank freely of it. I saw all was over with him, that I
could do no more for him. I left him to

struggle alone in the dark with none to soothe or comfort and I have always indulged the hope that an angel carried his noble and brave soul beyond the conflict of armies and the cruelty of war.

There was yet another touching incident in this night ramble among the dead. I had a private soldier, W. C. Robinson, in my Company. He was the son of an old itinerant Methodist preacher of the Alabama Conference. I called out "15 Alabama" and not far off he answered, "here". I asked "Is this you Billy?" He said, "Yes". I said, "Are you much hurt?" He replied, "I am killed." I found a minie ball had passed through the body and that his statement was too true. He said, "Who holds the battlefield". He faced danger with the chivalry of the bravest knight and death with the placidity of the bravest Christian.

I was on the second Maurn battleground ten days after the battle. No Federal soldiers had been buried. They were in a state of putrefaction and were distended almost to the condition of bursting. Thousands of these poor fellows lay on the ground, in some places I could have walked for hundreds of yards on the dead and Federal troops had turned as black as a Negro which they invariably did in a few hours after they were killed. It was a phenomena the Confederates did not turn black. This was not only a dreary, revolting spectacle, but seen just at night, was a frightful sight.

I saw an old excavation cut in a railroad, hundreds of Yankee soldiers killed together not covered with earth.

The confederates had been buried, but in a small clump of oak trees I found one confederate soldier. Evidently he had been dead but a few hours and, no doubt, he died from neglect and starvation. I paused, looked at the little pile of bones and emaciated manhood and in the sympathy of my soul said here lies a noble dead, perhaps brave and good and yet no marble slab will ever mark his resting place and no wife or mother will ever learn of his painful and lingering death.

The battleground was under a flag of truce and that night I slept in some house with at least a dozen volunteers and army surgeons.

We waded the Potomac River to get to the Battle of Gettysburg and returning crossed on pontoons. There are some facts in this battle I have not seen in history. The 15th Alabama Regiment was the extreme right of General Lee's. Just as we began the attack Hood was wounded and Law took command of the division. Our regiment crept over Big Round Top Mountain and fought until all our ammunition was exhausted and for want of reinforcement and ammunition was compelled to retire.

In this battle I saw General Bulger shot through the body. He fell like a dead man and after the war I met the same gentleman. He was a candidate for Governor of the State of Alabama.

I saw Colonel Oates, since Governor of Alabama, mount a rock within thirty yards of the enemy and discharge the contents of a repeater in their face.

When we began the retreat back across the mountains the Federals were pressing and I was exhausted and with my third lieutenant and private soldier, slipped into a cave in the side of the mountain and about midnight came out, located the pickets by the firing and crowded between their post which was about a hundred yards apart and reached our command in safety. I am satisfied I went as far toward Washington as any other Southern soldier.

On many of our campaigns we often waded rivers from waist to neck deep and that we might stem the current we walked, four abreast, and with arms around each other, constituted mutual support. I had a very narrow escape at Suffolk on the southern side of Richmond. I was in command of a long line of pickets and had the advantage of a dense line of timber that covered us from view of the enemy. The line was at least eight hundred yards long and my left wing gave way while I was at the right and I ran in between my own men and the enemy who had then entered the woods and had driven my forces back. I found myself within a hundred yards of a solid line of Federal Soldiers, but as the woods were dense I do not think they ever saw me. I found my command had secured a good position about five hundred yards back and quietly awaited my coming.

The army began its retreat at dark and I was left on duty with orders to withdraw at one A.M. sharp and cover the retreat to Black Water, twenty-five miles, which I did without loss of a man and in perfect order. In that fight I lost several of my best men. One soldier whose name was Cameron was killed and my detailed cook, Jesse Flowers*, carried him back to a camp and his body now rests in an old field pine thicket near Suffolk, Virginia. Flowers met me on his return with his sleeves rolled up to his elbows and said, "Captain, they have killed my old mess mate and best friend and I am now ready to fight until they kill me or I kill some of them." Soon the news came to me that Jesse Flowers was killed. By the side of his friend they buried him. Two braver soldiers never shouldered a musket or wore the Confederate gray. I wish I could indulge in the hope that they might arise with the just. But Flowers was wicked and Cameron, I think, was not religious, so I throw the mantle of oblivion over these two men and await the revelation of the great hereafter.

The three best friends I had in the army or ever had, all met their death in the same way. One was Lieutenant Patten who took camp fever at Manassas in 1861 and was transferred to a hospital at Richmond and soon I received notice he was dead. He was a gentleman of intelligence and a friend that never faltered or flickered. When he left I felt like I should never see him again and too soon my forebodings were realized. He was a wicked man and the last word I ever heard from him before the final farewell was an oath. It is probable he may have had a death bed repentance and from his narrow and crude little bunk gone up to a wider and better berth.

The second was John Trawick. I detailed him as a cook. He was shot accidentally in the foot in the valley near Harper's Ferry and died in a hospital at Winchester. John Trawick was a poor man, illiterate, unmannerly, profane and dissipated and yet he would do more for me and my comfort than any man living or dead. After the hardest wars and battles he would never sleep, though we might not reach camp until 12 or 1 o'clock at night, until he had prepared my supper, no matter how I protested. I am ashamed to say after the lapse of thirty years how much Mr. Trawick did for me.

Florence was the third and as I have already spoken freely of him, I will let that suffice.

My work as missionary was to the troops of Florida. My headquarters were scattered from the mouth of the Sewanee River to St. Andrews Bay, from Marian to the nearest point on the coast was from fifty to sixty miles and there was but one human habitation between.

I took my wife and oldest child on one trip. We stayed all night at the midway house. It was a pole hut, twelve by fourteen; one room, besides my family there was another family of eleven persons and I have never yet found out how we all slept as the night was cold. One thing I remember, the man took quite a fancy to Mrs. Edwards and gave her a fine venison ham as we returned home.

There were many dense thickets or "Tight Eye Swamps" in all that country and served as an impregnable fortress for hostile deserters. I never passed one of these that I did not feel I was in great danger. I expected to hear the deserters' rifles from these thickets every time I passed them. I suffered far more uneasiness than I did in the regular army.

Returning from one of my tours to the post at St. Andrews Bay I met an army composed of Yankees, Negroes and deserters, they raided Marian, burned a part of the town and killed some of its citizens. It was ten miles out they leveled their guns on me. I thought as I had no weapon and was outnumbered I had better surrender. They carried me ten miles further towards the coast and then took my horse, the best one I ever owned, and turned me loose on foot with a pair of heavy saddle pockets and seventy miles from home and twenty from anywhere else. On foot I started home. Almost the entire way either exposed to danger from the deserters or negroes loafing around, whose owners had run out of the country and they were imprudently occupying it.

In going from my home in south Alabama to the troops in Florida I had a stopping place with a Mrs. Clark. One evening just before sundown I met her and her little girl about two miles from her house. She told me I had better turn back that

300 deserters were camped at her house and they would either kill or badly mistreat me if I went on. I asked her if she could take care of me, she said she would try. I turned, rode back to her sister's and they held a consultation and decided to send or carry me to Mrs. Reed's, a deserter's wife, who lived in the lone pine woods back from the public road. These ladies said if the deserters came to Mrs. Reed's she would claim me as her guest and save me. Mrs. Reed agreed to take me and do the best she could for me. She lived in a pole cabin with open cracks as large as your arm. She fed me that night on boiled sweet potatoes which was the best and all she had for my horse was peas. It was a bright moonlight night, here was a brilliant fire of lightwood on the hearth and I sat leaning back by a large crack in the chimney corner. I looked out and saw a line of deserters at least a hundred armed with shotguns and muskets coming right to my back. I asked the lady if it would not be safer if I moved. She said that would create suspicion and cause them to stop and if I did not move they would most likely pass on. I don't think I ever sat so still before or since or covered so little space. That night they attacked the county seat, Newton, fifteen miles away. Four were killed and so many wounded.

After the surrender there were marauders robbing and hanging men friendly to the war and supposed to have money and I had been told I would share a similar fate. So we gave our valuables to our cook, Hogue, among other things a $150.00 gold watch and I took a Negro boy, Lewis, a bed quilt and shotgun and went out in a thicket near the house determined if they came to have the advantage of being on the outside. After we had been up for about an hour I said, "Lewis, I will go to sleep and you watch and if anybody comes you wake me." "Yes, sah, Marse Billy, if any man hurts you this night he will have to first walk over my dead body."

I went to sleep and woke the next morning with Lewis sleeping by my side, enjoying a full share of the quilt with me. I never asked Mrs. Edwards how she spent the night, but I guess she was as good to the cook as I was to Lewis. This was the last uneasy night I ever spent on account of war.

The last transaction I ever had in Confederate money I sold a calf skin for $300.00.

I was, at one time, offered a position on the weather bureau with a salary of $1,500.00 and the rank of captain if I would be mustered into service. I declined it. There were times when I had flattering prospects as a preacher, but that is all gone now. I once had offers and temptations to other pursuits, but that is all gone.

An Arab once rode a fine horse in front of an English officer and the Englishman offered him such tempting prices for his animal he galloped away from it to get out of his reach.

So I have gone out of the way of temptations. I have not done it as the Arab, but Old Time has mounted me and has rode me beyond the flattering offers and temptations of the world and now I keep my eye on the mark for the prize of the high calling of God in Christ Jesus.

****

Thirty years have passed. I am ninety years old today.

I have broken the family record.

My father died at 82 and my mother at 76, a pretty fair record for longevity. Besides my immediate family I have forty-five grandchildren.

One thing dominated me as far back as I can remember, a determination never to grow old, that is never to have old folk's ways, to be a boy in spirit through life and I do not think I have ever risen much above a boy in any respect. I suppose I have been what the world would call an optimist, that is, a man that hasn't anything and doesn't want anything. I think I had my duplicate in an old farmer in Alabama. He had forty acres of $3.00 per acre of land, and a possum dog and said he would not take forty thousand dollars for it. To me every picture of life has two sides and I have always turned the bright side to my gaze. I have always taken a forward look. The fate of Lot's wife early impressed me with the backward look.

I have preferred Paul's rule of action, forgetting the things that are behind.

Seventy-two years ago I joined the Methodist Church and my name was never off the church roll or the conference roll since.

I have been preaching sixty-four years and in all these years I have done many things I should not have done and left many things undone.

I think I can say today before the Good Father in whose presence I must soon appear I have always been loyal to Christ. I have confessed Him before me. I have taken the Christian side of every moral issue in life that has come before the public for action.

I joined the Alabama Conference and filled pastorates there as follows: Central Institute, Autaugaville, Ivey Creek, Summerfield and Day. I remained in that conference ten years, then transferred to the North Texas Conference, November 17, 1875. Served the Sulphur Springs Circuit; and Greenville Station. Located in December, 1876. For several years I taught school near Greenville, 1876 to 1880. Farmersville, 1880 to 1884. Lewisville, 1884 to 1886.

In 1886 I was readmitted into the North Texas Conference. My pastoral charges were Collinsville, Mt. Pleasant, Atlanta, Kaufman, Wills Point, Cochran and Caruth, Royse City, Fate, West Dallas, Haskell Avenue and Princeton. Fifty years of my ministry was spent in Texas and thirty-five years of this time was spent preaching in and around Dallas. I have seen the M. E. Church South grow from 455,000 members to two and one quarter million.

On March 1, 1925, I was made Chaplain General of the Trans-Mississippi Department of the United Confederate Veterans which was a distinctive honor to me.

I am proud of my country, my church, and my family and the age in which I live.
****

My father passed away on December 12, 1926. He had reached the age of 91 years and 10 months.

He preached on his 90th birthday at the Oak Lawn Methodist Church on Cedar Springs and Oak Lawn Avenue.

On his 91st birthday, February 28, 1925, he preached at the Oak Cliff Methodist Church on Jefferson Street.

He was looking forward to preaching at the invitation of Dr. Gregory at First Methodist Church on the corner of Ross Avenue and Harwood on his 99th birthday. He preached at Lakewood Methodist Church just one week before his death.
He was a frequent writer to the Texas Christian Advocate and to the Dallas Morning News.

 A friend has said of him:

"Brother Edwards had all the charm of a cultured Christian gentleman. He was a reader of good books. He thought out the fundamental questions. He wrote with ease and always illuminatingly. He prepared thoroughly his own discourses and he expected the preacher to whom he listened to give a message of strength and clearness. He lived here far beyond the limit of most men, but he lived to the last with full purpose. He was loved and cherished in his own home and by his brethren and friends. He passed on to his glorious crown with God's grace, resting upon him and with peace and good will abounding towards all men. We shall see him again."

Mrs. George A.
Cochran 2019 Bowser
Avenue Dallas, Texas

More About William Archibald Edwards and Eliza Jones White:
Marriage License: 04 Jan 1858 in Russell County, Alabama
Marriage Fact: Married by John C. Ardis, M.G.

v.	Mary Clementine Edwards, daughter of Ambrose Edwards and Emeline James Gaulding was born on 06 Dec 1836 in Talbot County, Georgia. She died on 27 Sep 1871 in Statesville, Alabama. She married Mordecai White, son of Theophilus White

and Mary H. Jett on 17 Mar 1853. He was born on 02 Sep 1829 in Brunswick
County, Georgia. He died on 06 Jan 1896 in Autauga County, Alabama.

More About Mary Clementine Edwards:
Burial: Love Family Cemetery, Mulberry, Autauga County, Alabama

Notes for Mary Clementine Edwards:
Died of burns received while protecting her children when a kerosene
lamp exploded.

More About Mordecai White:
Burial: Love Family Cemetery, Mulberry, Autauga County,
Alabama Cause Of Death: pneumonia
Occupation: 1850 in Russell County, Alabama; Teaching
Occupation: 1860 in Dale County, Alabama; Clerk
Occupation: 1870 in Henry County, Alabama; Dry Goods Merchant
Occupation: 1892 ; Member of State Legislature from Autauga County,
Alabama
Military Service: Bet. 02 Mar-23 Dec 1863; Company I, 57th Alabama Infantry,
C.S.A.

Notes for Mordecai White:

Served as Captain of Company I, 57th Alabama Infantry from March 21, 1863
until he resigned for health reasons on December 23, 1863.

Headstone has his name as Mordica White.
----

    vi.   Sarah E. Edwards, daughter of Ambrose Edwards and Emeline James
Gaulding was born on 06 Aug 1838 in Talbot County, Georgia. She died in Jun
1849 in Alabama.

8.   vii. Ambrose Newton Edwards, son of Ambrose Edwards and Emeline James Gaulding was
born on 21 Oct 1840 in Russell County, Alabama. He died on 20 Jul 1933 in Strawn,
Texas. He married Joanna Columbia Ardis, daughter of Isaac Ardis and Jane
Elizabeth White on 05 Dec 1865 in Dale County, Alabama. She was born on
4 Feb 1847 in Salem, Alabama. She died on 08 Aug 1922 in Greenville, Texas.

    ix.   Young Mansfield Edwards, son of Ambrose Edwards and Emeline James Gaulding
was born in May 1843 in Russell County, Alabama. He died on 22 Feb 1923 in
Sulphur Springs, Hopkins County, Texas. He married Martha E. Ardis, daughter of
Archibald McCoy Ardis and Joanna Leticia White on 05 Dec 1865 in Dale County,
Alabama. She was born on 25 Feb 1843 in Russell County, Alabama. She died on
27 Jan 1903 in Brazoria County, Texas.

More About Young Mansfield Edwards:
Burial: 22 Feb 1923 in City Cemetery, Sulphur Springs, Texas, 1C, Lot
40
Cause Of Death: Kidney Failure (Brights Disease)
Occupation: 1870 in Bright Star, Texas (present day Sulphur Springs,
Texas); School Teacher

Occupation: 1880 in Sulphur Springs, Texas; Merchant
Occupation: 1900 in Brazoria County, Texas; Farmer
Occupation: 1910 in Brazoria County, Texas; Farm Laborer
Occupation: 1920 in Sulphur Springs, Texas; None, living with his brother in
law, Henry Love Ardis.
Military Service: Bet. 03 Jul 1861-09 Apr 1865; Company E. 15th Alabama
Infantry, C.S.A.

Notes for Young Mansfield Edwards:
     Captured near Knoxville, Tennessee November 29, 1863 and imprisoned at
Fort Delaware. Exchanged on October 10, 1864 and rejoined Company E, 15th
Alabama Infantry, serving until the surrender of the Army of Northern Virginia at
Appomattox Court House.

     Enlisted in Company E, 15th Alabama Infantry at Fort Mitchell, Alabama on
July 3, 1861.

     Engagements: Winchester, Cross Keys, Cold Harbor, Malvern Hill, Cedar
Mountain, Hazel River, Second Manasses Junction, Chantilly, Harper's
Ferry, Sharpsburg, Fredricksburg, Suffolk, Battle Mount, Chicamauga,
Raccoon Mountain, Lookout Valley, Camel Station, Knoxville.

     Wounded at Sharpsburg.and Fredricksburg.

     Pre War residence was Westville, Alabama

     Had no children.

More About Martha E. Ardis:
Burial: City Cemetery, Sulphur Springs, Texas, 1C, Lot 39

Notes for Martha E. Ardis:
Filed a claim with the Confederate War Department on November 17, 1863 for
the loss of her first husband, William B. Moore.
----

ix.   James Carter Edwards, son of Ambrose Edwards and Emeline James Gaulding
       was born on 20 Sep 1844 in Russell County, Alabama. He died about 1854.

x.   Charles Anderson Brown Edwards, son of Ambrose Edwards and Emeline James
       Gaulding was born on 25 Oct 1846 in Russell County, Alabama. He died on 23
       Dec 1937 in Dothan, Alabama. He married Martha Caroline Crittenden, daughter
       of Cincinnatus Decatur Crittenden and Emeline Amanda Mahone on 01 Sep 1867
       in Ozark, Alabama. She was born on 09 Feb 1851 in Schley County, Georgia.
       She died on 04 Apr 1929 in Ozark, Alabama.

More About Charles Anderson Brown Edwards:
Burial: 24 Dec 1937 in Morning View Cemetery, Ozark,
Alabama
Occupation: 1870 in Dale County, Alabama; Farmer
Occupation: 1880 in Daleville, Dale County, Alabama; Farmer
Occupation: 1900 in Daleville, Dale County, Alabama; Farmer
Occupation: 1910 in Ozark, Alabama; Farmer

Occupation: Bet. 16 Jan 1911-16 Jan 1917 in Dale County, Alabama;
Probate Judge
Occupation: 1920 in Ozark, Alabama; Retired
Occupation: 1930 in Ozark, Alabama; Retired
Military Service: Bef. Feb 1864 ; Company A., Goldson's Alabama Battalion
Military Service: Bet. Feb 1864-05 May 1865 ; Company A, Brown's
Independent Cavalry, Davidson's Battalion, Alabama Cavalry
Property: 1870 in Dale County, Alabama; 100 Acres Improved and 230
Acres Unimproved

Notes for Charles Anderson Brown Edwards:
Served two terms in the Alabama state legislature from Dale County; 1887-
1889 and 1890-1891.

Paroled after Civil War: May 5, 1865 at Eufaula, Alabama.

More About Martha Caroline Crittenden:
Burial: 05 Apr 1929 in Morning View Cemetery, Ozark, Alabama

Notes for Martha Caroline Crittenden:
"Caroline" is the spelling used in the 1860 U.S. census.
----

xi.   Walter Starr Edwards, son of Ambrose Edwards and Emeline James Gaulding
was born on 09 Sep 1850 in Russell County, Alabama. He died on 21 Sep 1927
in Geneva, Geneva County, Alabama. He married Sarah Frances Brown on 08
Jan 1871. She was born on 10 May 1853 in Georgia. She died on 30 May 1920
in Enterprise, Alabama.

More About Walter Starr Edwards:
Burial: Enterprise City Cemetery, Enterprise, Alabama
Occupation: 1870 in Westville, Dale County, Alabama; School Teacher
Occupation: 1880 in Westville, Dale County, Alabama; Farmer
Occupation: 1892 Superintendent of Education, Coffee County, Alabama. Elected
August 1, 1892 and commissioned August 25, 1892.
Occupation:1894 in Coffee County, Alabama; County Superintendant of
Education. Elected August 6, 1894 and commisioned September 25, 1894.
Occupation: 1900 in Enterprise, Alabama; Timber Agent
Occupation: 1903; Notary Public, Enterprise, Alabama. Appointed February
28, 1903 and commissioned March 6, 1903.
Occupation:1910 in Enterprise, Alabama; Life Insurance
Agent
Occupation: 1920 in Enterprise, Alabama; City Clerk
Property: 1880 in Dale County, Alabama; 65 Acres Improved and 70
Acres Unimproved

Notes for Walter Starr Edwards:
Death record gives Geneva, Geneva County, Alabama as place of death.

More About Sarah Frances Brown:

18.   **Isaac Ardis**, son of John Ardis and Martha Stallings was born in 1816 in Greene County, Georgia. He died in 1870 in Sulphur Springs, Texas. He married **Jane Elizabeth White**, daughter of Johnathan White and Elizabeth (unknown) on 19 Oct 1842 in Russell County, Alabama.

19.   **Jane Elizabeth White**, daughter of Johnathan White and Elizabeth (unknown) was born on 27 Aug 1825 in Meriwether County, Georgia. She died on 21 Sep 1905 in Strawn, Texas.

More About Isaac Ardis:
Living In: 1840 Russell County, Alabama
Occupation: 1850 in Russell County, Alabama; Farmer
Occupation: 1860 in Pike County, Alabama; Farmer
Property: 1850 in Russell County, Alabama; 200 Acres Improved and 120 Acres Unimproved

Notes for Isaac Ardis:
Became a Mason at Brightstar Lodge number 221 in Sulphur Springs, Texas on December 3, 1868. Obituary for his wife states that Isaac died in 1870, indicating that it was probably early 1870. Isaac is not with his wife and children on the 1870 U.S. census for Hopkins County, Texas dated August 17, 1870.

Isaac Ardis died in 1870 before August 17, 1870 when the 1870 U.S. census for Precinct 1, Hopkins County, Texas was enumerated.

More About Jane Elizabeth White:
Burial: Mount Marion Cemetery, Strawn, Texas
Living In: 1870 Hopkins County, Texas on the farm of Thomas Beard
Living In: 1900 Young County, Texas with her son Julius C. Ardis and family.
Occupation: 1880 in Hopkins County, Texas; Farmer

Notes for Jane Elizabeth White:

     Strawn, Tex., Sept. 21 - Mrs. E.J. Ardis died at the residence of A.N. Edwards this morning at 8 o'clock. Deceased was 80 years old and had lived in Texas many years. She leaves eight children, Dr. I. Ardis of Greenville, three sons at Eliasville, two sons at Sulphur Springs, Mrs. T. Marshall of Indian Territory, and Mrs. A.N. Edwards of this place." 23 Sep 1905, The Dallas Morning News, page 7.

More About Isaac Ardis and Jane Elizabeth White:
Marriage License: 19 Oct 1842 in Russell County, Alabama
Marriage Fact: 28 Feb 1842 ; Marriage Bond signed
Marriage Fact: Married by John W. Tally, M.G.

Jane Elizabeth White and Isaac Ardis had the following children:

     i.   John C. Ardis, son of Isaac Ardis and Jane Elizabeth White was born on 11 Mar 1843 in Salem, Alabama. He died on 06 Sep 1858 in Pike County, Alabama.

    ii.   Julius Caesar Ardis, son of Isaac Ardis and Jane Elizabeth White was born in 1845 in Salem, Alabama. He died in 1863 in Iuka, Tishomingo County, Mississippi.

More About Julius Caesar Ardis:
Military Service: Bet. 10 Jan-17 Nov 1863 ; Company E, 53rd Alabama
Mounted Infantry, C.S.A.

9. iii. Joanna Columbia Ardis, daughter of Isaac Ardis and Jane Elizabeth White was born on 04 Feb 1847 in Salem, Alabama. She died on 08 Aug 1922 in Greenville, Texas. She married Ambrose Newton Edwards, son of Ambrose Edwards and Emeline James Gaulding on 05 Dec 1865 in Dale County, Alabama. He was born on 21 Oct 1840 in Russell County, Alabama. He died on 20 Jul 1933 in Strawn, Texas.

 iv. Johnathan White Ardis, son of Isaac Ardis and Jane Elizabeth White was born in Apr 1850 in Salem, Alabama. He died on 11 May 1917 in San Antonio, Bexar County, Texas. He married Rosa Lee Brinker on 21 Nov 1875 in Sulphur Springs, Texas. She was born in Apr 1853 in Shelby County, Alabama. She died on 27 Jun 1919 in Sulphur Springs, Hopkins County, Texas.

More About Johnathan White Ardis:
Burial: City Cemetery, Sulphur Springs, Texas
Cause Of Death: Chronic Nephritis and Arteriosclerosis
Occupation: 1870 in Hopkins County, Texas; Working on
farm.
Occupation: 1880 in Hopkins County, Texas; Farmer
Occupation: 1900 in Sulphur Springs, Hopkins County, Texas; Cotton Buyer
Occupation: 1910 in Sulphur Springs, Hopkins County, Texas; Cotton Buyer

More About Rosa Lee Brinker:
Burial: 30 Jun 1919 in City Cemetery, Sulphur Springs, Hopkins County, Texas Cause Of Death: Disentery
Notes for Rosa Lee Brinker:
Ardis, White, Mrs. - died last Sunday after a lingering illness and remains were buried in the City Cemetery, with funeral services being conducted by Pastor Mood of the First Methodist Church of which the deceased had been a long devout member. She was buried beside her husband who died May 1917. She was 65 years old, having been born in Alabama in 1854, and lived in Hopkins County for the past 45 years. In 1875, she was married to J.W. Ardis. To this union were born three children as follows: Mrs. J. Manly Carter of Chickasha, OK, Louis Ardis of Sulphur Springs, and Dollie Ardis who died early in Life. (Hopkins Co. Echo, July 4, 1919).

 v. Isaac Ardis, son of Isaac Ardis and Jane Elizabeth White was born on 16 Dec 1851 in Salem, Alabama. He died on 13 Apr 1913 in Greenville, Texas. He married Martha J. Taylor, daughter of Alexander Taylor and Margaret Davis on 05 Dec 1875 in Hunt County, Texas. She was born on 18 Oct 1843 in Marshall County, Tennessee. She died on 07 Feb 1923 in Greenville, Texas.

More About Isaac Ardis:
Burial: 13 Apr 1913 in East Mount Cemetery, Greenville,
Texas
Occupation: 1870 in Hopkins County, Texas; Working on
farm.
Occupation: 1880 in Hunt County, Texas; Doctor
Occupation: 1900 in Hunt County, Texas; Druggist
Occupation: 1910 in Hunt County, Texas; Medical Practitioner

Notes for Isaac Ardis:
Headstone has December 16, 1851 for date of birth. Death certificate
has December 16, 1850 for date of birth.

Listed in Directory of Deceased American Physicians.

More About Martha J. Taylor:
Burial: 08 Feb 1923 in East Mount Cemetery, Greenville, Texas
Cause Of Death: Arteriosclerosis

vi.   Robert Henry Ardis, son of Isaac Ardis and Jane Elizabeth White was born on
21 Jan 1854 in Salem, Alabama. He died on 17 Dec 1932 in Eliasville, Texas.
He married Amanda A. Wells, daughter of William Wells and (unknown) Carver
on 27 Dec 1877 in Sulphur Springs, Texas. She was born on 11 Mar 1859 in
Sulphur Springs, Texas. She died on 26 Oct 1926 in Eliasville, Texas.

More About Robert Henry Ardis:
Burial: 18 Dec 1932 in Eliasville Cemetery, Eliasville, Texas
Occupation: 1880 in Hopkins County, Texas; Farmer
Occupation: 1900 in Throckmorton County, Texas; Farmer
Occupation: 1910 in Young County, Texas; Farmer
Occupation: 1920 in Young County, Texas; Farmer
Occupation: 1930 in Young County, Texas; Retired

More About Amanda A. Wells:
Burial: 28 Oct 1926 in Eliasville Cemetery, Eliasville,
Texas
Cause Of Death: Apoplexy

vii.   William Howard Ardis, son of Isaac Ardis and Jane Elizabeth White was born on
23 Apr 1856 in Pike County, Alabama. He died on 18 Sep 1924 in Eliasville,
Texas. He married Edna Earl Collins, daughter of Henry Clay Collins and Mary
Ann Darwin in 1885 in Greenville, Hopkins County, Texas. She was born on 07
Apr 1868 in Tennessee. She died on 09 Jan 1907 in Eliasville, Texas.

More About William Howard Ardis:
Burial: Oak Grove Cemetery, Graham, Texas
Living In: 1900 Young County, Texas
Occupation: 1880 in Hopkins County, Texas; Working on his mother's
farm
Occupation: Bet. 20 Oct 1891-22 Jun 1894 ; Postmaster, Eliasville, Texas
Occupation: 1900 in Young County, Texas; General Merchant
Occupation: 1910 in Young County, Texas; Farmer
Occupation: 1920 in Terry County, Texas; Farmer

More About Edna Earl Collins:
Burial: Oak Grove Cemetery, Graham, Texas

viii.   John C. Ardis, son of Isaac Ardis and Jane Elizabeth White was born on 11 Dec 1858 in Pike County, Alabama. He died on 09 Oct 1860 in Pike County, Alabama.

ix.   James E. Ardis, son of Isaac Ardis and Jane Elizabeth White was born on 09 Jul 1861 in Westville, Alabama. He died on 24 Sep 1934 in Sulphur Springs, Texas. He married Clistia Ellen Chapin, daughter of Paul Stilman Chapin and Matilda (unknown) on 22 Aug 1883 in Sulphur Springs, Texas. She was born on 22 Aug 1866 in Sulphur Springs, Texas. She died on 24 Mar 1934 in Sulphur Springs, Texas.

More About James E. Ardis:
Burial: 25 Sep 1934 in Gafford Chapel Cemetery, Hopkins County, Texas
Cause Of Death: Peritonitis
Occupation: 1880 in Hopkins County, Texas; Farming with his mother.
Occupation: 1900 in Hopkins County, Texas; Farmer
Occupation: 1920 in Sulphur Springs, Hopkins County, Texas; Farmer
Occupation: 1930 in Hopkins County, Texas; Farmer

Notes for James E. Ardis:

Ardis, J. E. -1861 -1934 (Obituary)
J. E. Ardis, age 73, passed away Monday afternoon, Sept. 24, 1934, at the home of his daughter, Mrs. Dowe Harris, at Overland, following a stroke Saturday night. His wife passed away exactly six months ago. He is survived by two daughters, Mrs. Nonnie Russell, Commerce, and Mrs. Vergoe Harris, Overland; one son, Julius Ardis, of Gafford Chapel, and one brother, Julius, of California. One daughter, Miss Omar (sic) Ardis, passed away seven years ago. Funeral services and burial were held at Gafford's Chapel, conducted by Dr. J. Sam Barcus. He was a native of Kentucky and came to Texas with his father's family early in life and settled in Gafford's Chapel community where he has lived over half a century. (Hopkins Co. Echo, Sept. 28, 1934)
(NOTE: James E. Ardis was from Alabama not Kentucky.)

More About Clistia Ellen Chapin:
Burial: 24 Mar 1934 in Gafford Chapel Cemetery, Hopkins County, Texas
Cause Of Death: Heart Failure

Notes for Clistia Ellen Chapin:
Headstone has 1867 for year of birth. Death certificate has August 22, 1866 for date of birth.

x.   Julius Caesar Ardis, son of Isaac Ardis and Jane Elizabeth White was born on 02 Feb 1864 in Westville, Alabama. He died on 14 Jul 1937 in Breckenridge, Stephans County, Texas. He married Cora Densmore, daughter of Samuel M. Densmore and Margaret C. (unknown) on 18 Nov 1895 in Eliasville, Texas. She was born on 20 Jan 1870 in Greene County, Tennessee. She died on 17 Nov 1910 in Eliasville, Texas.

More About Julius Caesar Ardis:
Burial: 15 Jul 1937 in Eliasville Cemetery, Eliasville, Texas
Cause Of Death: Cerebral Hemorrhage
Living In: 1930 Living with his brother, Robert Henry Ardis, in Young County, Texas.
Occupation: 1880 in Hopkins County, Texas; Working on his mother's farm.
Occupation: 1900 in Young County, Texas; General Merchandise
Occupation: 1910 in Young County, Texas; Farmer
Occupation: 1920 in Hockley County, Texas; Rail Road Section Laborer
Occupation: 1930 in Eliasville, Texas; Retired

More About Cora Densmore:
Burial: Eliasville Cemetery, Eliasville, Texas

xi.　Martha Inez Ardis, daughter of Isaac Ardis and Jane Elizabeth White was born on 09 Aug 1866 in Greenville, Alabama. She died on 23 Jun 1911 in Lamar County, Texas. She married Thomas H. Marshall, son of John L.Marshall and Susan A. (unknown) on 05 Dec 1883 in Lamar County, Texas. He was born in Aug 1863 in Arkansas.

More About Thomas H. Marshall:
Occupation: 1900 in Hopkins County, Texas; Farmer
Occupation: 1910 in Antlers, Pushmataha County, Oklahoma; Farmer

---

Generation 6

32.　**William Newton Edwards**, son of Ambrose Edwards and Jemima (unknown) was born about 1773 in Orange County, North Carolina. He died in 1855 in Russell County, Alabama. He married **Mary Whatley**, daughter of Michael Whatley and Hannah Rhodes in 1798 in Talbot County, Georgia.

33.　**Mary Whatley**, daughter of Michael Whatley and Hannah Rhodes was born about 1776 in Orange County, North Carolina. She died in 1850 in Dale County, Alabama.

More About William Newton Edwards:
Living In: 1830 Talbot County, Georgia
Living In: 1840 Talbot County, Georgia
Living In: 1850 Living with his son, Wilson B. Edwards, in Russell County, Alabama Military
Service: Second Regiment, Beaufort County, North Carolina Militia, War of 1812

Notes for William Newton Edwards:
Living with his son, Wilson B. Edwards, in the 1850 Russell County, Alabama, U.S. census with age listed as 77 years old and birth place as North Carolina.

Mary Whatley and William Newton Edwards had the following children:
　　i.　James Young Edwards, son of William Newton Edwards and Mary Whatley was born on 20 Aug 1799 in Wilkes County, Georgia. He died on 13 Jun 1879 in Lee County, Alabama. He married Mary Perdue on 20 Jun 1822 in Jones County,

Georgia. She was born on 08 Nov 1801 in Georgia. She died on 21 May 1865 in Lee County, Alabama. He married Eliza Dunlap on 31 Aug 1865 in Russell County, Alabama. She was born in 1814 in South Carolina. She died on 26 Dec 1873 in Lee County, Alabama. He married Lauticia Taylor, daughter of Thomas Taylor on 29 Oct 1876 in Lee County, Alabama. She was born about 1845 in Georgia.

More About James Young Edwards:
Cause Of Death: Pneumonia
Living In: 1830 Talbot County, Georgia
Living In: 1840 Talbot County, Georgia
Living In: 1866 Russell County, Alabama
Occupation: 1850 in Russell County, Alabama; Farmer
Occupation: 1860 in Russell County, Alabama; Farmer
Occupation: 1870 in Salem, Lee County, Alabama; Farmer
Property: 1850 in Russell County, Alabama; 100 Acres Improved and 60 Acres Unimproved
Property: 1860 in Russell County, Alabama; 200 Acres Improved and 80 Acres Unimproved
Property: 1880 in Lee County, Alabama; 100 Acres Improved and 60 Acres Unimproved

Notes for James Young Edwards:
Moved from Talbot County Georgia to Russell County, Alabama in 1844. This part of Russell County is now in Lee County, Alabama.

There is a June 1880 Productions of Agriculture report that shows Young Edwards having 100 Acres Improved and 60 Acres Unimproved in Lee County, Alabama. Possibly this is his estate.

1880 property record is from 1880 Lee County Productions of Agriculture that was posted after his death.

Lived in Bibb County, Georgia after his first marriage and moved to Talbot County, Georgia in 1827. Moved to Russell County, Alabama in 1844.

Notes for Mary Perdue:
Rev. Cherry in "The History of Opelika" gives Mary's date of death as May 21, 1865.

Rev. Cherry in "The History of Opelika" gives her last name as Perdien but marriage record has Purdue.

More About James Young Edwards and Mary Perdue:
Marriage License: 20 Jun 1822 in Jones County, Georgia
Marriage Fact: Married by D. T. Milling, J.P.

More About James Young Edwards and Eliza Dunlap:
Marriage License: 28 Aug 1865 in Russell County, Alabama
Marriage Fact: Married by M. Y. Britt, M.G.

More About Lauticia Taylor:
Living In: 1880 Salem, Lee County, Alabama

Notes for Lauticia Taylor:
Rev. Cherry in "The History Of Opelika" gives marriage date as October 20, 1876.

Spelling of her first name is from her signature on her husband's probate records.

More About James Young Edwards and Lauticia Taylor:
Marriage Fact: Marriage performed by J. H. Lockhart

ii.   Nancy Edwards, daughter of William Newton Edwards and Mary Whatley was born on 12 Aug 1801 in Georgia. She died about 1883 in Texas. She married Phillip M. Long on 20 Jun 1819 in Jones County, Georgia.

More About Nancy Edwards:
Living In: 04 Jun 1880 With her grandson, J.A. Crouch, and his family in Harrison County, Texas.

More About Phillip M. Long:
Living In: 1830 Talbot County, Georgia

More About Phillip M. Long and Nancy Edwards:
Marriage License: 18 Jun 1819 in Jones County,
Georgia Marriage Fact: Married by H. Candler, J.P.

iii. John Edwards, son of William Newton Edwards and Mary Whatley was born on 04 Mar 1803 in Georgia. He died in 1857 in Talbot County, Georgia. He married Mary Oliver. She was born about 1808 in Georgia. She died in 1872 in Talbot County, Georgia.

More About John Edwards:
Burial: Edwards Cemetery, Talbotton, Georgia
Living In: 1830 Talbot County, Georgia
Living In: 1840 Talbot County, Georgia
Occupation: 1850 in Talbot County, Georgia; Farmer

More About Mary Oliver:
Burial: Edwards Cemetery, Talbotton, Georgia
Occupation: 1860 in Talbotton, Talbot County, Georgia; Farmer
Occupation: 1870 in Talbotton, Talbot County, Georgia; Farmer
Property: 1860 in District 685, Talbot County, Georgia; 300 Acres Improved and 90 Acres Unimproved
Property: 1870 in Talbot County, Georgia; 300 Acres Improved and 100 Acres Unimproved

16.   iv. Ambrose Edwards, son of William Newton Edwards and Mary Whatley was born on 16 Apr 1805 in Wilkes County, Georgia. He died on 06 Oct 1884 in Dale County,

Alabama. He married Emeline James Gaulding, daughter of John Gaulding and Martha Gaulding in 1827 in South Carolina. She was born on 10 Feb 1810 in Virginia. She died on 01 Jan 1886 in Dale County, Alabama.

v. William Edwards, son of William Newton Edwards and Mary Whatley was born on 28 Jan 1807 in Georgia.

vi. Michael Edwards, son of William Newton Edwards and Mary Whatley was born on 24 Mar 1810 in Georgia. He died in 1854 in Russell County, Alabama. He married Matilda Adams on 01 Oct 1837 in Talbot County, Georgia. She was born on 20 Dec 1821 in North Carolina. She died on 03 Mar 1901 in Alabama.

More About Michael Edwards:
Occupation: 1840 in Talbot County, Georgia; Farmer
Occupation: 1850 ; Farmer, Russell County, Alabama
Property: 1850 in Russell County, Alabama; 30 Acres Improved and 60 Acres Unimproved

More About Matilda Adams:
Burial: Leon Cemetery, Leon, Crenshaw County, Alabama
Living In: 1900 Living with John A. Hollis and his family in Leon, Crenshaw County, Alabama.

More About Michael Edwards and Matilda Adams:
Marriage Fact: Married by Robert Fleming (MG)

vii. Jemima Edwards, daughter of William Newton Edwards and Mary Whatley was born in Jan 1813 in Georgia. She died in Alabama. She married Ezekiel Brown on 21 Aug 1831 in Talbot County, Georgia.

More About Ezekiel Brown and Jemima Edwards:
Marriage Fact: Married by Hiram Powell (MG)

viii. Mary Edwards, daughter of William Newton Edwards and Mary Whatley was born on 16 May 1815 in Georgia. She died before 18 Feb 1875 in Alabama. She married William Robinson. He was born about 1815. He died before 25 Jan 1850. She married William C. Cleghorn on 08 Sep 1852 in Russell County, Alabama. He was born on 22 Apr 1832 in Hall County, Georgia. He died on 19 Jul 1910 in Macon County, Alabama.

More About Mary Edwards:
Occupation: 1850 in Russell County, Alabama; Farmer

More About William C. Cleghorn:
Burial: Pleasant Springs Baptist Church Cemetery, Franklin, Macon County, Alabama
Occupation: 1860 in Russell County, Alabama; Farmer
Occupation: 1880 in Tuskegee, Macon County, Alabama; Farmer
Occupation: 1900 in Franklin, Macon County, Alabama; Farmer

Occupation: 1910 in Macon County, Alabama; Farmer
Military Service: Bet. 25 Jul 1863-1865 in Opelika, Alabama; Enlisted in
Company H, 61st Alabama Infantry, C.S.A.

More About William C. Cleghorn and Mary Edwards:
Marriage Fact: Married by John Bevin J.P.

ix.   Elizabeth Edwards, daughter of William Newton Edwards and Mary Whatley was
      born about 1818 in Georgia. She died after 03 Jun 1880. She married William
      Trotter, son of William Trotter and (unknown) on 28 Dec 1843 in Talbot County,
      Georgia. He died in 1848. She married Felston Parker on 19 Dec 1849 in
      Russell County, Alabama. He was born on 12 Dec 1815 in North Carolina. He
      died before 09 Aug 1870.

      More About Elizabeth
      Edwards: b: 1817
      Living In: 1850 Russell County, Alabama with her second husband, Felston
      Parker
      Living In: 1860 Russell County, Alabama
      Living In: 1870 Opelika, Lee County, Alabama
      Living In: 1880 Pierce Chapel, Lee County, Alabama

      Notes for William Trotter:
      William Trotter died young and William's father was made guardian of his children.

      More About William Trotter and Elizabeth Edwards:
      Marriage License: 28 Dec 1843 in Talbot County, Georgia
      Marriage Fact: Married by Charles A. Brown (M.G.)

      More About Felston Parker:
      Occupation: 1850 in Russell County, Alabama; Farmer
      Occupation: 1860 in Russell County, Alabama; Farmer

      More About Felston Parker and Elizabeth Edwards:
      Marriage Contract: 18 Dec 1849 in Russell County, Alabama

x.   Spencer Edwards, son of William Newton Edwards and Mary Whatley was born
      on 03 Apr 1817 in Georgia. He died on 02 Nov 1897 in Taylor County, Georgia.
      He married Mary Ann Willis, daughter of John E. Willis and Susanna H. Biggs on
      25 Apr 1836 in Talbot County, Georgia. She was born about 1821 in Georgia. She
      died before 1880.

      More About Spencer Edwards:
      Burial: Butler City Cemetery, Butler, Taylor County,
      Georgia
      Living In: 1866 Dale County, Alabama
      Living In: 1880 Living with his son James R. Edwards, and his family in Westville,
      Dale county, Alabama
      Occupation: 1850 in Talbot County, Georgia; Farmer

Occupation: 1860 in Talbot County, Georgia; Farmer
Occupation: 1870 in Dale County, Alabama; Farmer
Occupation: 1883 in Haw Ridge, Alabama; Constable - Appointed
and commissioned March 7, 1883.
Occupation: 1888 in Precinct 13, Coffee County, Alabama; Justice of the Peace
- Elected August 6, 1888.
Military Service: Indian War of 1836
Property: 1850 in Talbot County, Georgia; 35 Acres Improved and 15
Acres Unimproved
Property: 1852 in Talbot County, Georgia; 150 Acres
Property: 1856 in Talbot County, Georgia; 95 Acres
Property: 1860 in Talbot County, Georgia; 35 Acres Improved and 15
Acres Unimproved
Property: 1870 in Dale County, Alabama; 200 Acres Improved and 200
Acres Unimproved

Notes for Spencer Edwards:
Died while visiting A. J. Fountain in Taylor County, Georgia.

More About Mary Ann Willis:
b: Abt. 1821

More About Spencer Edwards and Mary Ann Willis:
Marriage Fact: Married by G. B. Clay (J.P.)

    xi.   Wilson B. Edwards, son of William Newton Edwards and Mary Whatley was born on
27 Jun 1821 in Georgia. He died on 16 Sep 1863 in Russell County, Alabama. He
married Eleanor Aurora Trotter, daughter of William Trotter and (unknown) on 10 Aug
1843. She was born on 11 Apr 1823 in Russell County, Alabama. She died on
27 Oct 1873.

More About Wilson B. Edwards:
Occupation: 1850 in Russell County, Alabama; Farmer
Occupation: 1860 in Russell County, Alabama; Farmer
Property: 1850 in Russell County, Alabama; 30 Acres Improved and 30 Acres
Unimproved
Property: 1860 in Russell County, Alabama; 175 Acres Improved and 115 Acres
Unimproved

Notes for Wilson B. Edwards:
Died in the Civil War.

Estate was probated in Russell County, Alabama. Probate documents indicated
his death was between August 1, 1863 and December 14, 1863.
----

34.   **John Gaulding**, son of Archibald Gaulding was born about 1780 in Virginia. He died about 1839
in Mobile, Alabama. He married **Martha Gaulding**, daughter of Jesse Gaulding on 14 Apr 1808
in Prince Edward County, Virginia.

35. **Martha Gaulding**, daughter of Jesse Gaulding was born about 1788 in Virginia. She died on 14 Jan 1827 in Bibb County, Georgia.

More About John Gaulding:
Cause Of Death: Yellow Fever

Martha Gaulding and John Gaulding had the following children:

i. Archibald Alexander Gaulding, son of John Gaulding and Martha Gaulding was born about 1808 in Virginia. He died on 08 Aug 1870 in Atlanta, Georgia. He married Frances Ann Horton, daughter of Josiah Horton on 30 Dec 1830 in Monroe County, Georgia. She was born on 01 Nov 1816 in Virginia. She died on 27 Sep 1858. He married Sallie G. (unknown) before 14 Jun 1860. She was born about 1820 in Georgia.

More About Archibald Alexander Gaulding:
Burial: Oak Hill Cemetery, Griffin, Georgia
Cause Of Death: Consumption (Tuberculosis)
Living In: 1840 Monroe County, Georgia
Living In: 1850 Pike County, Georgia
Living In: 1870 Atlanta, Fulton County, Georgia
Occupation: 1847 Legislator for Pike County, Georgia
Occupation: 1860 in Atlanta, Fulton County, Georgia; Editor
Occupation: Bet. 17 Aug-22 Nov 1861 ; Surveyor General of Georgia
Occupation: Proprietor and Editor of the Atlanta Intelligencer newspaper.
Occupation: Publisher of "The Empire State" newspaper in Spalding County, Georgia.
Military Service: 22 Dec 1834; Captain of "Monroe Blues" in Monroe County, Georgia.

Notes for Archibald Alexander Gaulding: 9 August 1870

The Atlanta Constitution
Atlanta Georgia

Col Archibald A. Gaulding died in this city yesterday, in the 64th year of his age a victim of consumption. Col. Gaulding was a man of benevolent nature He stood high in the Masonic Fraternity, occupied during his life many responsible public stations, in 1847 was a member of the Legislature from Pike County, subsequently held the offices of Surveyor-General of the State and Auditor of the State Road, was for several years one of the proprietors and editor of the Empire State, and subsequently one of the proprietors and editors of the Atlanta Intelligencer upon the editorial staff of which he was employed at the time of his decease. Holding offices of high trust in the State, he discharged the duties they imposed upon him acceptably and faithfully. His remains were sent to Griffin yesterday evening for interment. He giveth the weary rest.

More About Frances Ann Horton:
Burial: Oak Hill Cemetery, Griffin, Georgia

More About Archibald Alexander Gaulding and Frances Ann Horton:
Marriage Fact: Married by Reverend Thomas Battle.

More About Sallie G. (unknown):
Living In: 1870 Atlanta, Fulton County, Georgia
Living In: 1880 Atlanta, Fulton County, Georgia

17.   ii. Emeline James Gaulding, daughter of John Gaulding and Martha Gaulding was born on 10 Feb 1810 in Virginia. She died on 01 Jan 1886 in Dale County, Alabama. She married Ambrose Edwards, son of William Newton Edwards and Mary Whatley in 1827 in South Carolina. He was born on 16 Apr 1805 in Wilkes County, Georgia. He died on 06 Oct 1884 in Dale County, Alabama.

iii. Clementine E. Gaulding, daughter of John Gaulding and Martha Gaulding was born about 1812 in Georgia. She married Francis F. Nunn, son of William Nunn on 21 Dec 1826 in Monroe County, Georgia. He was born about 1801 in Georgia. He died before 1856 in Mississippi.

More About Clementine E. Gaulding:
Living In: 1850 Chickasaw County, Mississippi
Living In: 1860 Calhoun County, Mississippi
Living In: 1880 Living in the household of her son in law, James Woodrell, and his family in Muddy Bayou, Faulkner County, Arkansas.

More About Francis F. Nunn:
Occupation: 1850 in Chickasaw County, Mississippi; Farmer

More About Francis F. Nunn and Clementine E. Gaulding:
Marriage Fact: Married by Reverend P. Oglethorp

iv. Salina Gaulding, daughter of John Gaulding and Martha Gaulding was born about 1818 in Georgia. She married Stephen S. Taylor. He was born about 1816 in Virginia.

More About Salina Gaulding:
Occupation: 1860 in District 1001, Spalding County, Georgia; Milliner

More About Stephen S. Taylor:
Occupation: 1850 in District 68, Pike County, Georgia; Clerk
Occupation: 1860 in District 1001, Spalding County, Georgia; Clerk

v. Arianne Gaulding. She died in Indianola, Texas. She married John Coates.

36.   **John Ardis**, son of Isaac Ardis and Mary Howell was born on 01 Dec 1793 in Beech Island, South Carolina. He died on 04 Aug 1878 in Greenville, Alabama. He married **Martha Stallings**, daughter of Malachi Stallings and Martha Moseley on 11 Aug 1811 in Greene County, Georgia.

37.   **Martha Stallings**, daughter of Malachi Stallings and Martha Moseley was born on 08 Feb 1787 in York County, South Carolina. She died on 18 Nov 1855 in Salem, Alabama.

More About John Ardis:
b: 01 Dec 1793
Burial: Pioneer Cemetery, Greenville, Alabama
Living In: 1820 Putnam County, Georgia
Living In: 1840 Russell County, Alabama
Living In: 1850 Russell County, Alabama
Living In: 1866 Butler County, Alabama
Living In: 1870 Greenville, Butler County, Alabama
Occupation: 1850 in Russell County, Alabama; Farmer
Property: 1850 in Russell County, Alabama; 220 Acres Improved and 140 Acres Unimproved

More About Martha Stallings:
b: 08 Feb 1787
Burial: Salem, Alabama

Martha Stallings and John Ardis had the following children:

i.   Mary Ann McCoy Ardis, daughter of John Ardis and Martha Stallings was born on 30 Mar 1812 in Greene County, Georgia. She died on 16 Jan 1850 in Harris County, Georgia. She married Stephen C. Pace, son of William Pace and Mary May on 10 Jul 1827 in Putnam County, Georgia. He was born on 11 Jul 1802 in South Carolina. He died on 14 Apr 1872 in Creek Stand, Macon County, Alabama.

More About Mary Ann McCoy Ardis:
Burial: Pace Cemetery, Columbus, Muscogee County, Georgia

More About Stephen C. Pace:
b: 11 Jul 1802
Burial: Creek Stand Cemetery, Creek Stand, Macon County, Alabama
Occupation: 1850 in Harris County, Georgia; Farmer
Occupation: 1860 in Macon County, Alabama; Farmer
Occupation: 1870 in Warrior Stand, Macon County, Alabama; Farmer

Notes for Stephen C. Pace:
DEATH AND OBITUARY NOTICES FROM THE SOUTHERN CHRISTIAN ADVOCATE Issue of May 8, 1872 -- Stephen Pace died at his residence at Creek Stand, Macon county, Ala., April 14th 1872. Brother Pace was born in Edgefield District, South Carolina, July 11th 1802. his father removed to Putnam county, Ga., when he was a child. In 1828, brother Pace moved to Harris county, Ga., where he remained until 1854, when he removed to the place where he died.
----

18.   ii. Isaac Ardis, son of John Ardis and Martha Stallings was born in 1816 in Greene County, Georgia. He died in 1870 in Sulphur Springs, Texas. He married Jane

Elizabeth White, daughter of Johnathan White and Elizabeth (unknown) on 19 Oct 1842 in Russell County, Alabama. She was born on 27 Aug 1825 in Meriwether County, Georgia. She died on 21 Sep 1905 in Strawn, Texas.

iii. Archibald McCoy Ardis, son of John Ardis and Martha Stallings was born on 28 Aug 1818 in Putnam County, Georgia. He died on 02 May 1859 in Greenville, Alabama. He married Joanna Leticia White, daughter of Johnathan White and Elizabeth (unknown) on 28 Feb 1842 in Russell County, Alabama. She was born in 1826 in Oglethorpe, Georgia.

More About Archibald McCoy Ardis:
Burial: Greenville, Alabama
Occupation: 1850 in Russell County, Alabama; Farmer
Property: 1850 in Russell County, Alabama; 100 Acres Improved and 80 Acres Unimproved

Notes for Archibald McCoy Ardis:
Living in Russell County, Alabama in 1850.

More About Joanna Leticia White: b: 1826
Living In: 1860 Living in Pike County, Alabama next door to her brother in law, Isaac Ardis.
Living In: 1870 Joanna and her children (John, Isaac and Henry) are living with her son in law, Young Mansfield Edwards, in Hopkins County, Texas

iv. Caroline Columbia Sarah Ann Collingsworth Ardis, daughter of John Ardis and Martha Stallings was born on 18 Nov 1821 in Putnam County, Georgia. She died on 21 Feb 1910 in Corsicana, Navarro County, Texas. She married John Pace, son of William Pace and Mary May on 02 Feb 1835 in Harris County, Georgia. He was born on 09 Dec 1809 in Putnam County, Georgia. He died on 17 Nov 1879 in Corsicana, Navarro County, Texas.

More About Caroline Columbia Sarah Ann Collingsworth Ardis:
Burial: 22 Feb 1910 in Ennis, Ellis County, Texas
Living In: 05 Jun 1880 Caroline and her daughter, Martha, are living with Caroline's son, John Ardis Pace, in Ellis County, Texas
Living In: 09 Jun 1880 Caroline and her daughter, Martha, are living with Caroline's son, Stephen A. Pace, in Corsicana, Texas

More About John Pace:
b: 07 Dec 1809
Burial: Myrtle Cemetery, Ennis, Ellis County, Texas
Cause Of Death: Typhoid Fever
Occupation: 1850 in Muscogee County, Georgia; Farmer
Occupation: 1860 in Russell County, Alabama; Farmer
Occupation: 1870 in Salem, Lee County, Alabama; Farmer

v. Julius Ardis, son of John Ardis and Martha Stallings was born about 1820 in Putnam County, Georgia.

vi.   John Columbus Ardis, son of John Ardis and Martha Stallings was born on 31 Aug
        1823 in Putnam County, Georgia. He died on 24 Dec 1877 in Downey, California. He
        married Frances Amanda Harris, daughter of Britain D. Harris and Sarah A.
        Walton on 17 Apr 1848 in Russell County, Alabama. She was born on 23 Nov
        1831 in Alabama. She died on 01 Dec 1902 in Downey, California.

        More About John Columbus Ardis:
        Burial: Downey District Cemetery, Downey, California
        Occupation: 1850 in Russell County, Alabama; Lawyer
        Occupation: 1860 in El Dorado, Union County, Arkansas; School Teacher
        Occupation: 1870 in Los Nietos, Los Angeles County, California; School
        Teacher
        Occupation: Minister

        Notes for John Columbus Ardis:
        Graduated from Emory College in Oxford, Georgia in
        1846.
        Licensed to preach by John W. Starr in 1847.
        Moved to Union County, Arkansas in 1859.
        Ordained a Deacon in the Methodist Episcopal Church, South by Bishop Andrew
        in 1856.
        Ordained as elder by Bishop Paine in 1860.
        Arrived in Los Angeles County, California in July 1868.

        More About Frances Amanda Harris:
        Burial: Downey District Cemetery, Downey, California
        Living In: 1900 Downey, Los Angeles County, California
        Occupation: 1880 Los Nietos, Los Angeles County, California; Farmer

        More About John Columbus Ardis and Frances Amanda
        Harris:
        Marriage Fact: Married by J. Sciafe, M.G.

vii.   Martha Aly D. Ardis, daughter of John Ardis and Martha Stallings was born on 25 Apr
        1825 in Putnam County, Georgia. She died on 07 Aug 1906 in Vernon Parish,
        Louisiana. She married Anderson V. Allen about 1844 in Russell County, Alabama. He
        was born about 1821 in Russell County, Alabama. He died on 20 Nov 1846. She
        married Charner T. Scaife on 01 Mar 1848 in Russell County, Alabama. He was born
        about 1823 in South Carolina. He died on 09 Jun 1858 in Atlanta, Georgia.
viii.
        More About Martha Aly D. Ardis:
        Burial: Old Leesville Cemetery, Leesville, Vernon Parish, Louisiana
        Living In: 1860 With her children, in Salem, Russell County, Alabama.
        Living In: 1870 With her children, in Dale County, Alabama
        Living In: 1880 Pensacola, Florida in the household of Green Brown, father
        in law of her son, John Scaife.
        Living In: 1900 With her son, William Scaife, and his family in Dead Fall,
        Butler County, Alabama.

        Notes for Anderson V. Allen:
        Estate probated in Russell County, Alabama. Administrator of his estate was
        John Ardis.

More About Charner T. Scaife:
Occupation: 1850 in Russell County, Alabama; Merchant

viii.   Elizabeth Ardis, daughter of John Ardis and Martha Stallings was born in 1828 in Columbus, Georgia. She died before 10 Jul 1860. She married George W. Adair, son of John D. Adair and Mary P. (unknown) on 20 Jul 1847 in Russell County, Alabama. He was born in 1829 in Gwinnett County, Georgia.

More About Elizabeth Ardis:
Cause Of Death: Consumption (Tuberculosis)

More About George W. Adair:
Occupation: 1850 in Russell County, Alabama; Farmer
Occupation: 1860 in Smackover Township, Ouachita County, Arkansas; Farmer

More About George W. Adair and Elizabeth Ardis: Marriage Fact: Married by J. Scaife, M.G.

ix.   Wiley Hamil Ardis, son of John Ardis and Martha Stallings was born on 08 May 1830 in Columbus, Georgia. He died on 22 Jan 1892 in Carthage, Panola County, Texas. He married Frances L. Miller, daughter of John Miller on 09 Nov 1848 in Chambers County, Alabama. She was born in 1829 in Georgia. She died on 30 Mar 1885 in Texas. He married Demetsia J. Higgins on 12 Jul 1887 in Panola County, Texas.

More About Wiley Hamil Ardis:
Burial: Athens Cemetery, Athens, Henderson County, Texas
Occupation: 1850 in Russell County, Alabama; Farmer
Occupation: 1860 in Butler County, Alabama; Preacher
Occupation: 1870 in Fincastle, Henderson County, Texas; Minister of the Gospel
Occupation: 1880 in Fincastle, Henderson County, Texas; Minister
Military Service: Bet. 05 Apr-12 Aug 1862; Company E, 2nd Alabama Cavalry, C.S.A.

Notes for Wiley Hamil Ardis:
Enlisted in Company E, 2nd Alabama Cavalry at Bethel Church in Butler County, Alabama on April 5, 1862 as a private. Mustered in at Camp Stone on May 6, 1862. Horse valued at $300 by enlistment Officer at time of enlistment.
Became Chaplain of 2nd Alabama Cavalry on May 2, 1862.
Resigned his commision as Chaplain due to health on August 12, 1862.

1880 U.S. census shows Florence Early as an adopted daughter of Wiley and Frances Ardis and gives her name as Florence H. Ardis. Death certificate for Florence gives her name as Florence Early Grimes (wife of Edwin W. Grimes) and gives her parents names as Walter C. Early and Virginia F. Wilkinson.

More About Frances L. Miller:
Burial: Athens Cemetery, Athens, Henderson County, Texas

More About Wiley Hamil Ardis and Frances L. Miller:
Marriage Fact: Married by J. W. Starr, M.G.

38.   **Johnathan White**. He married **Elizabeth (unknown)**.

39.   **Elizabeth (unknown)**.

Elizabeth (unknown) and Johnathan White had the following children:

19.   i.   Jane Elizabeth White, daughter of Johnathan White and Elizabeth (unknown) was born on 27 Aug 1825 in Meriwether County, Georgia. She died on 21 Sep 1905 in Strawn, Texas. She married Isaac Ardis, son of John Ardis and Martha Stallings on 19 Oct 1842 in Russell County, Alabama. He was born in 1816 in Greene County, Georgia. He died in 1870 in Sulphur Springs, Texas.

          ii.   Joanna Leticia White, daughter of Johnathan White and Elizabeth (unknown) was born in 1826 in Oglethorpe, Georgia. She married Archibald McCoy Ardis, son of John Ardis and Martha Stallings on 28 Feb 1842 in Russell County, Alabama. He was born on 28 Aug 1818 in Putnam County, Georgia. He died on 02 May 1859 in Greenville, Alabama.

                More About Joanna Leticia
                White: b: 1826
                Living In: 1860 Pike County, Alabama next door to her brother in law, Isaac Ardis.
                Living In: 1870 Joanna and her children (John, Isaac and Henry) are living with her son in law, Young Mansfield Edwards, in Hopkins County, Texas

                More About Archibald McCoy
                Ardis: Burial: Greenville, Alabama
                Occupation: 1850 in Russell County, Alabama; Farmer
                Property: 1850 in Russell County, Alabama; 100 Acres Improved and 80 Acres Unimproved

                Notes for Archibald McCoy Ardis:
                Living in Russell County, Alabama in 1850.

Generation 7

64.   **Ambrose Edwards** was born about 1750 in Virginia. He died on 24 Feb 1823 in Jones County, Georgia. He married **Jemima (unknown)**.

65.   **Jemima (unknown)** was born about 1755. She died on 15 Dec 1823.

More About Ambrose Edwards:

Military Service: Revolutionary War - Served from Georgia.

Notes for Ambrose Edwards:
Recorded by D.A.R. as Revolutionary War veteran.

Georgia Archives, Drawer 186, Box 66.
Executor: brother John Edwards.

I Ambrose Edwards of the State County worn being weak of body though
in(perfect) mind and memory and knowing it is once appointed for all men once
to all doth make and ordain this my last will and testament. Item first I give
and bequeath to my (this space seems as to be written in Will Book B-the original
will reads "Negro woman Dinah her freedom") and appoint my son John Edwards
her Guardian during her life time and ten acres of land for her to life during her life
time adjoining the Cork and John Edwards receiving. I give to my beloved
daughter Sarah Lewis five dollars. I give and bequeath to the heirs of my daughter
Sarah Lewis body and equal proportion of my estate along the rest of my children.
Item the third I give and bequeath to my beloved daughter Elizabeth Bowen and
equal part of my estate among the rest of my children.
Item the fourth I give and bequeath to my beloved daughter Charity Campbell
and equal part of my estate among the rest of my children. Item the fifth I give
and bequeath to my beloved daughter Nancy Lewis and equal part of my estate
with the rest of my children. Item the sixth I give and bequeath to my beloved
son William Edwards and equal part of my estate with the rest of my children.
Item the Seventh I give and bequeath to my beloved son John Edwards and
equal part of my estate with the rest of my children and lastly I wish at the
expiration of the year for all my real and personal Estate to be sold that has
not been given away previously and an equal distribution to take place and I
do appoint and ordain John Edwards my only Executor of this my last will and
testament. In witness whereof I have herewith set my hand and seal this
twenty-fourth day of February in the year of our Lord 1823.
Witness: Ben Oliver, Jos. T. Dorough

Ambrose Edwards Seal and his Mark

Georgia the fourth of February marks term 1823. This day came before me in the
Court Joseph T. Dorough was being duly sworn vaitu himself with Ben Oliver
were sub serving witnesses to the long going will and that they by their equal of
the estate of Ambrose Edwards subscribe their in the presence of each other at
the home of his executor subscribed to me in open court this 3rd March 1823.

Joseph L. Dorough

JONES COUNTY GA Will Book A

Jemima (unknown) and Ambrose Edwards had the following children:
      i.   Mary Edwards, daughter of Ambrose Edwards and Jemima (unknown) was born
about 1770. She married William Whatley. He was born in 1767 in North
Carolina. He died in 1833.

      ii.   John Edwards, son of Ambrose Edwards and Jemima (unknown) was born about

1771 in North Carolina. He died in Jun 1863 in Chestnut Creek, Autauga County, Alabama. He married Margaret Whitehead on 10 Nov 1808 in Randolph County, Georgia (present day Jasper County). She died before 18 Dec 1815. He married Martha Weeks on 18 Dec 1815 in Jones County, Georgia.

More About John Edwards:
Burial: 05 Jun 1863 in Chestnut Creek, Autauga County, Alabama
Living In: 1850 Living with Charles Edwards and his family in Chestnut Beat, Autauga County, Alabama
Living In: 1860 Living with his daughter, Martha Thomas, and her family in Chestnut Creek, Autauga County, Alabama.

Notes for John Edwards:
Chestnut Creek, Autauga County, Alabama became part of Baker County, Alabama on April 30, 1868 when Baker County was formed. Baker County later changed its name to Chilton County.

There is a receipt for five dollars from John Miller in John Edward's probate records for transporting John's body to the grave on June 5, 1863.

On November 4, 1863 John's daughter, Martha. was made executor of his estate.

Loxla and Berry Edwards were born before John married Margaret Whitehead although John Edwards and Margaret Whitehead are frequently mentioned as their parents. Reverend Cherry does not mention who the parents of Loxla Edwards were in his book "The History of Opelika" although Reverend Cherry does mention the names of parents for Loxla's Edwards relatives mentioned in "The History of Opelika". Some pepple believe that Loxla and Berry might be illigitimate sons of one of John Edwards sisters. Perhaps John had an unknown wife before he married Margaret Whitehead.

More About John Edwards and Margaret Whitehead:
Marriage Fact: Married by Gilbert Barden, J.P.

More About John Edwards and Martha Weeks:
Marriage License: 16 Dec 1815 in Jones County, Georgia
Marriage Fact: Married by Daniel Melson, J.P.

32.   iii. William Newton Edwards, son of Ambrose Edwards and Jemima (unknown) was born about 1773 in Orange County, North Carolina. He died in 1855 in Russell County, Alabama. He married Mary Whatley, daughter of Michael Whatley and Hannah Rhodes in 1798 in Talbot County, Georgia. She was born about 1776 in Orange County, North Carolina. She died in 1850 in Dale County, Alabama.

iv. Sarah Edwards, daughter of Ambrose Edwards and Jemima (unknown) was born in 1780. She married John E. Lewis.

v. Elizabeth Edwards, daughter of Ambrose Edwards and Jemima (unknown) was born in 1782. She died in 1855 in Jackson County, Georgia. She married John Yarborough, son of Ambrose Yarborough about 1806. He was born in 1775. He died in 1822 in Hall County, Georgia. She married (unknown) Bowen.

vi. Charity Edwards, daughter of Ambrose Edwards and Jemima (unknown) was born in 1784 in Greene County, Georgia. She died in 1842. She married Samuel Campbell on 28 May 1801 in Greene County, Georgia. He was born about 1783 in Greene County, Georgia. He died in 1842.

vii.   Nancy Edwards, daughter of Ambrose Edwards and Jemima (unknown) was born on 01 Jan 1785 in Georgia. She died before 1850 in Russell County, Alabama. She married Henry Lewis, son of Richard Lewis and Carolyn Booker on 01 Jan 1807 in Greene County, Georgia. He was born on 11 Jun 1782 in Mecklinburg County, Virginia. He died after 1842.

More About Henry Lewis and Nancy Edwards:
Marriage License: 30 Dec 1806 in Greene County, Georgia
Marriage Fact: Married by J. Holt, J.P.

66.   **Michael Whatley**, son of Michael Whatley and Catherine Bird was born on 05 Jul 1750 in Culpepper County, Virginia. He died on 22 Aug 1840 in Henry County, Alabama. He married **Hannah Rhodes**, daughter of William Rhodes and Mary Baker in 1774 in North Carolina.

67.   **Hannah Rhodes**, daughter of William Rhodes and Mary Baker was born in 1753.

More About Michael Whatley:
Military Service: Revolutionary War, North Carolina

Notes for Michael Whatley:
Served from May 1780 until October 1780 in Captain Thompson's Company, Colonel Moore's North Carolina Regiment.
Served three months as a light horseman in Captain Hodges Company, Colonel O'Neals North Carolina Regiment.
Served three months as a spy for Colonel Taylor of North Carolina Troops. During this enlistment Michael was captured by the British while he was travelling from Orange county to Wilmington and was eventually paroled.

Hannah Rhodes and Michael Whatley had the following children:

33.   i. Mary Whatley, daughter of Michael Whatley and Hannah Rhodes was born about 1776 in Orange County, North Carolina. She died in 1850 in Dale County, Alabama. She married William Newton Edwards, son of Ambrose Edwards and Jemima (unknown) in 1798 in Talbot County, Georgia. He was born about 1773 in Orange County, North Carolina. He died in 1855 in Russell County, Alabama.

ii.   John Henry Whatley, son of Michael Whatley and Hannah Rhodes was born in 1779 in North Carolina. He died in 1855 in Henry County, Alabama. He married Polly Blanks, daughter of William Henry Blanks and Mariah Robertson on 24 Jun 1803 in Greene County, Georgia. She was born in 1790. She died in 1850. He married Elizabeth James on 18 Oct 1821 in Jasper County, Georgia. She was born in 1810 in Greene County, Georgia.

iii.   Nancy Whatley, daughter of Michael Whatley and Hannah Rhodes was born about 1774. She married Littleberry Watts on 21 Feb 1801 in Greene County, Georgia. He died in 1818 in Morgan County, Georgia.

iv.   Michael Whatley, son of Michael Whatley and Hannah Rhodes was born in Greene County, Georgia.

68.   **Archibald Gaulding**.

Archibald Gaulding had the following child:

34.   i.   John Gaulding, son of Archibald Gaulding was born about 1780 in Virginia. He died about
                  1839 in Mobile, Alabama. He married Martha Gaulding, daughter of Jesse Gaulding
                  on 14 Apr 1808 in Prince Edward County, Virginia. She was born about 1788 in
                  Virginia. She died on 14 Jan 1827 in Bibb County, Georgia.

70.   **Jesse Gaulding**.

Jesse Gaulding had the following children:

35.   i.   Martha Gaulding, daughter of Jesse Gaulding was born about 1788 in Virginia. She died
                  on 14 Jan 1827 in Bibb County, Georgia. She married John Gaulding, son of Archibald
                  Gaulding on 14 Apr 1808 in Prince Edward County, Virginia. He was born about 1780
                  in Virginia. He died about 1839 in Mobile, Alabama.

            ii.   Judith Gaulding, daughter of Jesse Gaulding was born about 1786.

            iii.   Joseph Gaulding.

            iv.   Elizabeth Gaulding, daughter of Jesse Gaulding was born about 1784.

            v.   Mary Gaulding.

            vi.   Lucy Gaulding.

            vii.   Nancy Gaulding.

            viii. John B. Gaulding.

72.   **Isaac Ardis**, son of Mathias Ardis and Christina Zinn was born in 1761 in Flat Creek, South
       Carolina. He died in 1795 in Beech Island, South Carolina. He married **Mary Howell**, daughter
       of Nathaniel Howell and Ann Nail about 1793 in Edgefield County, South Carolina.

73.   **Mary Howell**, daughter of Nathaniel Howell and Ann Nail was born in 1762. She died on 20
       Nov 1795 in Beech Island, South Carolina.

       More About Isaac Ardis:
       Burial: Beech Island, South Carolina
       Military Service: Revolutionary War, South Carolina Militia

       More About Mary Howell:
       Burial: Beech Island, South Carolina

       Mary Howell and Isaac Ardis had the following child:

36.   i.   John Ardis, son of Isaac Ardis and Mary Howell was born on 01 Dec 1793 in Beech
                  Island, South Carolina. He died on 04 Aug 1878 in Greenville, Alabama. He married
                  Martha Stallings, daughter of Malachi Stallings and Martha Moseley on 11 Aug 1811 in
                  Greene County, Georgia. She was born on 08 Feb 1787 in York County, South
                  Carolina. She died on 18 Nov 1855 in Salem, Alabama. He married Mary Jane
                  Trammel on 16 Dec 1856 in Butler County, Alabama. She was born on 06 Jan 1829 in
                  Georgia. She died in Feb 1901 in Van Buren County, Arkansas.

74.   **Malachi Stallings**, son of Jesse Lane Stallings and Winnifred Aycock was born in 1760 in Bertie,
       North Carolina. He died on 22 Mar 1803 in Greene County, Georgia. He married **Martha Moseley**.

75.   **Martha Moseley**, daughter of Robert Moseley and Mary (unknown) was born about 1760 in North Carolina. She died after 1803 in Greene County, Georgia.

More About Malachi Stallings:
Military Service: Revolutionary War, South Carolina Militia

Martha Moseley and Malachi Stallings had the following children:

37.   i.   Martha Stallings, daughter of Malachi Stallings and Martha Moseley was born on 08 Feb 1787 in York County, South Carolina. She died on 18 Nov 1855 in Salem, Alabama. She married John Ardis, son of Isaac Ardis and Mary Howell on 11 Aug 1811 in Greene County, Georgia. He was born on 01 Dec 1793 in Beech Island, South Carolina. He died on 04 Aug 1878 in Greenville, Alabama.

       ii.   Mary Stallings, daughter of Malachi Stallings and Martha Moseley was born about 1781. She died on 18 Sep 1823 in Putnam County, Georgia. She married Henry Chambers. He was born about 1769 in Rowan County, North Carolina. He died in 1802 in Greene County, Georgia. She married Archibald McKay. He died in 1824 in Putnam County, Georgia.

       iii. Susanna Stallings, daughter of Malachi Stallings and Martha Moseley was born on 25 Dec 1783 in Green County, Georgia. She died in Butler County, Alabama. She married Robert Reid, son of George Reid and Margaret Chambers before 1803. He was born on 20 Apr 1779 in Green County, Georgia. He died on 24 Apr 1813 in Putnam County, Georgia. She married James Lane on 12 Feb 1818 in Putnam County, Georgia.

       iv.   Reuben Stallings, son of Malachi Stallings and Martha Moseley was born about 1789 in Greene County, Georgia. He married Frances (unknown).

       v.   Sarah Stallings, daughter of Malachi Stallings and Martha Moseley was born on 22 Feb 1790 in Wilkes County, Georgia. She died on 17 May 1864 in Muscogee County, Georgia. She married Thomas Kimbrough on 27 Jan 1806 in Greene County, Georgia. He was born on 09 May 1788. He died on 10 Jul 1847 in Muscogee County, Georgia.

       vi.   Jesse Francis Stallings, son of Malachi Stallings and Martha Moseley was born on 24 Nov 1794 in Greene County, Georgia. He died on 06 Apr 1881 in Butler County, Alabama. He married Mary Mallory on 11 Mar 1813 in Greene County, Georgia. She was born on 09 Aug 1796 in Virginia. She died on 02 Dec 1879 in Butler County, Alabama.

       vii. William Daniel Stallings, son of Malachi Stallings and Martha Moseley was born on 11 Jul 1796 in Greene County, Georgia. He died on 13 Nov 1877 in Butler County, Alabama. He married Nancy Harriet Lane. She was born on 02 Mar 1802 in South Carolina. She died in 1846 in Butler County, Alabama. He married Bridget Williamson on 28 Feb 1848 in Pike County, Alabama. She was born on 30 Nov 1812 in Butler County, Alabama. She died about 1862 in Butler County, Alabama.

             More About William Daniel Stallings:
             Burial: Oakey Streak Cemetery, Butler County, Alabama

       viii. Grace Stallings, daughter of Malachi Stallings and Martha Moseley was born about 1802 in Greene County, Georgia. She died on 02 Aug 1870 in Muscogee County, Georgia. She married Henry Byrd Garrett on 20 Dec 1821 in Putnam County, Georgia. He was born about 1802 in Hancock County, Georgia. He died on 07 Mar 1853 in Muscogee County, Georgia.

ix.   Seby Stallings.

Generation 8

132.   **Michael Whatley**, son of Shirley Whatley and Rebecca B. Wharton was born on 22 Jul 1720 in Williamsburg, Hanover County, Virginia. He died on 24 Jul 1800 in Washington County, Georgia. He married **Catherine Bird**, daughter of John Bird and Mary (unknown) in 1741 in Hanover County, Virginia.

133.   **Catherine Bird**, daughter of John Bird and Mary (unknown) was born in 1725 in Virginia. She died in 1805 in Greene County, Georgia.

Notes for Michael Whatley:

      GA WILLS 1794-1810, p 13, Green Co GA, WA Co 16 Feb 1788, Probated 24 July 1800, Green Co. Michael Whatley
In the name of God, Amen. I Michael Whatley of the state of Georgia and county of Washington. I do make and ordain this my last Will and Testament in manner and form following.
First of all I do give and bequeath unto my Dearly Beloved wife, Catherine my hold estate for her maintenance during her life except a negro boy named Peter, a mahogany desk, a feather bed, a roan horse called Tryall, and the tract of land which I now live. I give to my youngest son Elisha the property above at the age of twenty one, and after decease of my wife. Remainder of my estate to be divided as follows: To Daughter, Franky Mason, a negro woman named Milly
To Son, Thomas Whatley, a negro girl named Jane
To Son, Jesse Whatley, a negro girl named Patt
To Daughter, Caty Morgan, a negro boy named Harry
To Gr/son, Hiram Whatley, son of Richard Whatley and Frances, his wife, a negro boy named Jim To Son, John Whatley, a horse valued to 10 pounds sterling to be paid out of my movable estate To Son, Richard Whatley, a cow and a calf to be paid likewise
To Son, Michael Whatley, a cow and a calf to be paid
likewise To Son, Daniel Whatley, feather bed and furniture.
All remainder of movable estate to be equally divided between my said Son, Daniel and Daughter Peggy Pickard, wife of John Pickard.

Executors: Sons Daniel Whatley and Elisha
Whatley Michael Whatley

(seal)

Catherine Bird and Michael Whatley had the following children:
66.   i.   Michael Whatley, son of Michael Whatley and Catherine Bird was born on 05 Jul 1750 in Culpepper County, Virginia. He died on 22 Aug 1840 in Henry County, Alabama. He married Hannah Rhodes, daughter of William Rhodes and Mary Baker in 1774 in North Carolina. She was born in 1753. He married Mary Thomas.

      ii.   Daniel Whatley, son of Michael Whatley and Catherine Bird was born on 25 Dec 1744 in Culpepper County, Virginia. He died on 28 Sep 1857 in Taylor County, Georgia. He married Mary Edwards. He married Amelia Barker.

            More About Daniel Whatley:
            Burial: Newsome   Cemetery,   Taylor   County,
            Georgia
            Military Service: Revolutionary War

      iii.   Frankie Whatley, daughter of Michael Whatley and Catherine Bird was born about 1746 in Virginia. She married Thomas Mason, son of John Mason in Georgia.

iv.   John Whatley, son of Michael Whatley and Catherine Bird was born about 1748 in Virginia. He died about 1805 in Greene County, Georgia. He married Mary Porter on 17 Mar 1789 in Greene County, Georgia. She was born after 1756.

v.   Thomas Whatley, son of Michael Whatley and Catherine Bird was born about 1753 in Virginia. He died about 1840. He married Ann (unknown).

vi.   Jesse Whatley, son of Michael Whatley and Catherine Bird was born about 1756 in North Carolina. He married Rachael Taylor.

vii.   Catherine Elizabeth Whatley, daughter of Michael Whatley and Catherine Bird was born about 1759 in North Carolina. She married James Morgan in 1784.

viii.   Margaret Whatley, daughter of Michael Whatley and Catherine Bird was born about 1763 in North Carolina. She died about 1821 in Orange County, North Carolina. She married John Richards.

ix.   Richard Whatley, son of Michael Whatley and Catherine Bird was born about 1766 in North Carolina. He married Frances Giles. She was born about 1783 in Wilkes County, Georgia.

x.   Elisha Whatley, son of Michael Whatley and Catherine Bird was born about 1769 in Warren County, North Carolina. He died on 10 Jul 1843 in Bibb County, Alabama. He married Thersey Gibbs in 1793 in Greene County, Georgia. She was born in 1770 in Jones County, Georgia. She died in 1835 in Bibb County, Alabama.

xi.   Nancy Whatley, daughter of Michael Whatley and Catherine Bird was born on 28 Feb 1770 in North Carolina. She died on 10 Nov 1852 in Lawrence County, Mississippi. She married Randall Huckaby Pierce in 1789. He was born on 27 Apr 1769. He died on 30 Aug 1853 in Lawrence County, Mississippi.

xii.   Ann Whatley, daughter of Michael Whatley and Catherine Bird was born in 1771. She married Stephen Richards.

134.   William Rhodes. He married **Mary Baker**.

135.   Mary Baker.

Mary Baker and William Rhodes had the following children:

67.   i. Hannah Rhodes, daughter of William Rhodes and Mary Baker was born in 1753. She married Michael Whatley, son of Michael Whatley and Catherine Bird in 1774 in North Carolina. He was born on 05 Jul 1750 in Culpepper County, Virginia. He died on 22 Aug 1840 in Henry County, Alabama.

ii.   Nancy Rhodes. She married (unknown) Gresham.

140.   John Gaulding. He married **Elizabeth Geer**.

141.   Elizabeth Geer.

Elizabeth Geer and John Gaulding had the following children:

70.   i.   Jesse Gaulding.

ii.   Jacob Gaulding.

144.   **Mathias Ardis** was born in Oct 1724 in Germany. He died on 09 Sep 1781 in Savannah, Georgia. He married **Christina Zinn**, daughter of Gerhardt Zinn and Margaretha Guth about 1755 in Flat Creek, South Carolina.

145.   **Christina Zinn**, daughter of Gerhardt Zinn and Margaretha Guth was born in 1725 in Neustadt, Germany. She died on 06 May 1785 in Beech Island, South Carolina.

Christina Zinn and Mathias Ardis had the following children:

72.   i. Isaac Ardis, son of Mathias Ardis and Christina Zinn was born in 1761 in Flat Creek, South Carolina. He died in 1795 in Beech Island, South Carolina. He married Mary Howell, daughter of Nathaniel Howell and Ann Nail about 1793 in Edgefield County, South Carolina. She was born in 1762. She died on 20 Nov 1795 in Beech Island, South Carolina.

ii.   Mary Ardis, daughter of Mathias Ardis and Christina Zinn was born in 1756 in Flat Creek, South Carolina. She died in 1804. She married John Bradley about 1771 in Beech Island, South Carolina. He was born on 19 Jan 1755. He died in 1782 in Savannah, Georgia. She married John DeYampert. He was born in 1755.

iii.   Matthias Ardis, son of Mathias Ardis and Christina Zinn was born about 1757 in Flat Creek, South Carolina.

iv.   Elizabeth Ardis, daughter of Mathias Ardis and Christina Zinn was born about 1758 in Flat Creek, South Carolina. She died before Oct 1783. She married Francis Carlisle.

v.   John Ardis, son of Mathias Ardis and Christina Zinn was born about 1759 in Flat Creek, South Carolina. He died before Oct 1783 in South Carolina.

vi.   Jacob Ardis, son of Mathias Ardis and Christina Zinn was born in 1763 in Flat Creek, South Carolina. He died in 1784 in South Carolina.

vii.   Sarah Ardis, daughter of Mathias Ardis and Christina Zinn was born in 1765 in Flat Creek, South Carolina. She died after 1827. She married Benjamin Bowers. She married Partain Purdue.

viii.   Abraham Ardis, son of Mathias Ardis and Christina Zinn was born in 1767 in New Windsor, South Carolina. He died on 30 May 1817 in Beech Island, , South Carolina. He married Susannah Shinholser, daughter of John Shinholser and Susannah Hiles about 1790 in Beach Island, South Carolina. She was born in 1774. She died on 15 Mar 1807 in Beech Island, , South Carolina. He married Sarah Rose Mary Zubley on 27 Apr 1809. She was born in 1773. She died on 03 Apr 1836 in Beech Island, , South Carolina.

More About Abraham Ardis:
Burial: Beech Island, , South Carolina

More About Susannah Shinholser:
Burial: Beech Island, South Carolina

More About Sarah Rose Mary Zubley:
Burial: Beech Island, South Carolina

ix.   Daniel Ardis, son of Mathias Ardis and Christina Zinn was born about 1768 in New Windsor, South Carolina.

x.   David Ardis, son of Mathias Ardis and Christina Zinn was born in 1773 in New Windsor, South Carolina. He died on 17 Oct 1800 in Beech Island, , South Carolina. He married Eleanor (unknown).

146.   **Nathaniel Howell**. He married **Ann Nail**.

147.   **Ann Nail**.

Ann Nail and Nathaniel Howell had the following child:

73.   i. Mary Howell, daughter of Nathaniel Howell and Ann Nail was born in 1762. She died on 20 Nov 1795 in Beech Island, South Carolina. She married Isaac Ardis, son of Mathias Ardis and Christina Zinn about 1793 in Edgefield County, South Carolina. He was born in 1761 in Flat Creek, South Carolina. He died in 1795 in Beech Island, South Carolina. She married James Richards on 01 Oct 1795.

148.   **Jesse Lane Stallings**, son of Elias Stallings and Susannah Arnold was born about 1721 in Bertie County, North Carolina. He died about 1804 in Burke County, Georgia. He married **Winnifred Aycock**.

149.   **Winnifred Aycock** was born in North Carolina. She died in Georgia.

More About Jesse Lane Stallings:

Military Service: Revolutionary War

Winnifred Aycock and Jesse Lane Stallings had the following children:

74.   i.   Malachi Stallings, son of Jesse Lane Stallings and Winnifred Aycock was born in 1760 in Bertie, North carolina. He died on 22 Mar 1803 in Greene County, Georgia. He married Martha Moseley. She was born about 1760 in North Carolina. She died after 1803 in Greene County, Georgia.

ii.   Jesse Lane Stallings, son of Jesse Lane Stallings and Winnifred Aycock was born about 1759 in Bertie County, North Carolina. He died before 20 Aug 1804 in Wilkes County, Georgia. He married Sarah Walker, daughter of Sanders Walker and Sarah Lamar Clinquefield about 1785 in Wilkes County, Georgia. She was born on 17 Mar 1769 in Wilkes County, Georgia.

iii.   John Stallings, son of Jesse Lane Stallings and Winnifred Aycock was born about 1761 in Bertie County, North Carolina. He married Mary (unknown).

iv.   Marianna Stallings, daughter of Jesse Lane Stallings and Winnifred Aycock was born about 1763 in Bertie County, North Carolina. She died in 1802 in Georgia. She married John McLean.

v.   Palasiah Stallings, son of Jesse Lane Stallings and Winnifred Aycock was born about 1767 in Georgia. He died after 1804. He married Mary Gordon.

vi.   Elizabeth Stallings, daughter of Jesse Lane Stallings and Winnifred Aycock was born about 1769 in Georgia. She died on 08 Mar 1803.

150.   **Robert Moseley**, son of William Moseley and Elizabeth (unknown) was born in 1725 in South Carolina. He died in 1796 in Edgefield County, South Carolina. He married **Mary (unknown)**.

151.   **Mary (unknown)**. She died before 12 Jan 1789.

More About Robert Moseley:
Military Service: Revolutionary War, South Carolina

Mary (unknown) and Robert Moseley had the following children:

75.   i.   Martha Moseley, daughter of Robert Moseley and Mary (unknown) was born about 1760 in North Carolina. She died after 1803 in Greene County, Georgia. She married Malachi Stallings. He was born in 1760 in Bertie, North carolina. He died on 22 Mar 1803 in Greene County, Georgia.

       ii.   Mary Moseley. She married Derrick Holsonback.

       iii.   John Moseley.

       iv.   Elizabeth Moseley. She married Edward Vann.

       v.   Sarah Moseley.

       vi.   Susannah Moseley.

       vii.   Edward Moseley, son of Robert Moseley and Mary (unknown) was born in 1771 in Edgefield District, South Carolina. He died in 1834 in Alabama. He married Martha Butler in 1793.

Generation 9

264.   **Shirley Whatley**, son of Samuel Whatley and Mary Shirley was born in 1685 in Jamestown, Virginia. He died on 27 Aug 1779 in Warren County, North Carolina. He married **Rebecca B. Wharton** in 1719 in Hanover County, Virginia.

265.   **Rebecca B. Wharton** was born in 1700 in Virginia. She died in 1785 in Wilkes County, Georgia.

More About Shirley Whatley:
Military Service: Granville N.C. Militia, 1734

Rebecca B. Wharton and Shirley Whatley had the following children:

132.   i.   Michael Whatley, son of Shirley Whatley and Rebecca B. Wharton was born on 22 Jul 1720 in Williamsburg, Hanover County, Virginia. He died on 24 Jul 1800 in Washington County, Georgia. He married Catherine Bird, daughter of John Bird and Mary (unknown) in 1741 in Hanover County, Virginia. She was born in 1725 in Virginia. She died in 1805 in Greene County, Georgia.

       ii.   Willis Whatley, son of Shirley Whatley and Rebecca B. Wharton was born in 1721 in Virginia. He died in 1799 in Hancock County, Georgia. He married Elizabeth Ann Green. She was born about 1725. He married Catherine Gennit. She was born about 1730.

       iii.   Wilson Whatley, son of Shirley Whatley and Rebecca B. Wharton was born about 1730. He died in 1776 in Wilkes County, Georgia. He married Mary Duke. She was born about 1730.

       iv.   Wharton Whatley, son of Shirley Whatley and Rebecca B. Wharton was born in 1734 in North Carolina. He died before 27 Mar 1798 in Wilkes County, Georgia. He married Elizabeth Garrett Madden. She was born in North Carolina. She died in Jul 1814 in Wilkes County, Georgia.

v.   Daniel Whatley, son of Shirley Whatley and Rebecca B. Wharton was born in 1744.

vi.   Ornan Bradley Whatley, son of Shirley Whatley and Rebecca B. Wharton was born on 08 May 1751 in North Carolina. He died on 01 Dec 1798 in Oglethorpe County, Georgia. He married Tabitha Green. She was born about 1755. He married Judith Thornton, daughter of John Thornton and Elizabeth (unknown) in 1769. She was born on 08 Feb 1751 in North Carolina. She died on 04 Nov 1842 in Paulding County, Georgia.

266.   **John Bird**. He married **Mary (unknown)**.

267.   **Mary (unknown)**.

Mary (unknown) and John Bird had the following child:
133.   i. Catherine Bird, daughter of John Bird and Mary (unknown) was born in 1725 in Virginia. She died in 1805 in Greene County, Georgia. She married Michael Whatley, son of Shirley Whatley and Rebecca B. Wharton in 1741 in Hanover County, Virginia. He was born on 22 Jul 1720 in Williamsburg, Hanover County, Virginia. He died on 24 Jul 1800 in Washington County, Georgia.

280.   **John Gaulding**. He married **Elizabeth (unknown)**.

281.   **Elizabeth (unknown)**.

Elizabeth (unknown) and John Gaulding had the following child:
140.   i.   John Gaulding. He married Elizabeth Geer.

290.   **Gerhardt Zinn** was born on 01 Mar 1704. He married **Margaretha Guth**.

291.   **Margaretha Guth** was born on 18 Dec 1702.

Margaretha Guth and Gerhardt Zinn had the following child:
145.   i. Christina Zinn, daughter of Gerhardt Zinn and Margaretha Guth was born in 1725 in Neustadt, Germany. She died on 06 May 1785 in Beech Island, South Carolina. She married Mathias Ardis about 1755 in Flat Creek, South Carolina. He was born in Oct 1724 in Germany. He died on 09 Sep 1781 in Savannah, Georgia.

296.   **Elias Stallings** was born about 1683 in Virginia. He died after 27 Mar 1763 in Bertie County, North Carolina. He married **Susannah Arnold**.

297.   **Susannah Arnold**.

Susannah Arnold and Elias Stallings had the following children:
148.   i. Jesse Lane Stallings, son of Elias Stallings and Susannah Arnold was born about 1721 in Bertie County, North Carolina. He died about 1804 in Burke County, Georgia. He married Winnifred Aycock. She was born in North Carolina. She died in Georgia.

ii.   Jacob Stallings, son of Elias Stallings and Susannah Arnold was born about 1711 in Bertie County, North Carolina.

iii. John Stallings, son of Elias Stallings and Susannah Arnold was born about 1713 in Bertie County, North Carolina. He married Priscilla (unknown).

iv.   Elias Stallings, son of Elias Stallings and Susannah Arnold was born about 1715 in Bertie County, North Carolina.

v.   Moses Stallings, son of Elias Stallings and Susannah Arnold was born about 1717 in Bertie County, North Carolina.

vi. Josiah Stallings, son of Elias Stallings and Susannah Arnold was born about 1723 in Bertie County, North Carolina. He died after 13 May 1772 in Bertie County, North Carolina. He married Mary Standley.

vii. Mary Stallings, daughter of Elias Stallings and Susannah Arnold was born about 1727 in Bertie County, North Carolina.

viii. Margaret Stallings, daughter of Elias Stallings and Susannah Arnold was born about 1729 in Bertie County, North Carolina.

ix. Susannah Stallings, daughter of Elias Stallings and Susannah Arnold was born about 1731 in Bertie County, North Carolina.

300. **William Moseley**. He married **Elizabeth (unknown)**.

301. **Elizabeth (unknown)**.

Elizabeth (unknown) and William Moseley had the following child:

150. i. Robert Moseley, son of William Moseley and Elizabeth (unknown) was born in 1725 in South Carolina. He died in 1796 in Edgefield County, South Carolina. He married Mary (unknown). She died before 12 Jan 1789. He married Penelope Talley.

Generation 10

528. **Samuel Whatley** was born in England. He died in 1740 in North Carolina. He married **Mary Shirley**.

529. **Mary Shirley**.

Mary Shirley and Samuel Whatley had the following child:

264. i. Shirley Whatley, son of Samuel Whatley and Mary Shirley was born in 1685 in Jamestown, Virginia. He died on 27 Aug 1779 in Warren County, North Carolina. He married Rebecca B. Wharton in 1719 in Hanover County, Virginia. She was born in 1700 in Virginia. She died in 1785 in Wilkes County, Georgia. He married Mary Cherrry in 1710 in Virginia. She was born about 1690. She died about 1718 in Virginia.

594. **Edward Arnold**.

Edward Arnold had the following child:

297. i. Susannah Arnold. She married Elias Stallings. He was born about 1683 in Virginia. He died after 27 Mar 1763 in Bertie County, North Carolina.